ACADEMIC LEADERSHIP DAY BY DAY

OTHER BOOKS BY JEFFREY L. BULLER

The Essential Department Chair: A Practical Guide to College Administration

The Essential Academic Dean: A Practical Guide to College Leadership

The Essential College Professor: A Practical Guide to an Academic Career

Classically Romantic: Classical Form and Meaning in Wagner's Ring

ACADEMIC LEADERSHIP DAY BY DAY

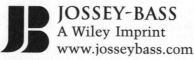

*Small Steps That Lead
to Great Success*

JEFFREY L. BULLER

JOSSEY-BASS
A Wiley Imprint
www.josseybass.com

Published by Jossey-Bass
A Wiley Imprint
989 Market Street, San Francisco, CA 94103-1741—www.josseybass.com

Jossey-Bass books and products are available through most bookstores. To contact Jossey-Bass directly call our Customer Care Department within the U.S. at 800-956-7739, outside the U.S. at 317-572-3986, or fax 317-572-4002.

Jossey-Bass also publishes its books in a variety of electronic formats. Some content that appears in print may not be available in electronic books.

Library of Congress Cataloging-in-Publication Data

Buller, Jeffrey L.
  Academic leadership day by day : small steps that lead to great success /
Jeffrey L. Buller.
     p. cm.
  Includes index.
  ISBN 978-0-470-90300-1 (pbk.); 9780470907597 (ebk); 9780470907948 (ebk);
9780470907962 (ebk)
  1. Educational leadership—United States. 2. Education, Higher—Effect of technological
    innovations on—United States. 3. College administrators—United States. I. Title.
  LB2341.B742 2010
  378.1'01—dc22   2010026650

Printed in the United States of America
FIRST EDITION

HB Printing   10 9 8 7 6 5 4 3 2 1

Contents

❖❖❖

October   33

November   67

Contents

Contents

March   *199*

Contents

Preface

Whenever I speak to leaders in higher education, they inevitably ask for ideas about how to handle the heavy workload of their jobs and manage their time better. They're always interested in learning ways to improve their academic leadership and become more effective; they just don't know when they'd ever find the time to read a book about academic leadership or to fit new approaches into their already overcrowded days. I have written *Academic Leadership Day by Day* with precisely this type of administrator in mind. The entries in this short guide have been created for several audiences:

- For academic leaders at all levels, from department chair and program director through chancellor and chief executive officer, I wanted to create an administrative equivalent to all those familiar books with titles like *Daily Thoughts for Daily Improvement* or *An Idea a Day to Streamline Your Life*. I must admit that I'm hopelessly addicted to books of this sort. I love the notion of taking a suggestion, boiling it down to its simplest form, and presenting it in a way that makes it useful to even the busiest people in only a few minutes each day.

- For administrators who believe that they need to turn their institutions upside down with continual change and the implementation of one grandiose strategy after another, I'd like to offer a rebuttal. If a school or program is facing a major disaster—economic collapse, severe enrollment decline, a scandal that landed it on the front page of the *Chronicle of Higher Education*, or something similar—then, by all means, go ahead and initiate a radical change, because channeling everyone's energy into a brand-new initiative is probably necessary. But not every problem is a crisis. As my friend Don Chu likes to say, not every problem is really a problem. For institutions that have been reasonably successful and just want to get better, diverting people's attention from their core tasks of teaching, scholarship, and service to focus on "strategic visioning," "repositioning," and inculcating a culture of continual, significant change is at the very least unnecessary. Even worse, the sense that everything about an institution must be constantly turned upside down can end up being highly destructive. There are plenty of little things that each of us can do to become better administrators, more effectively serve the needs of our stakeholders, increase our own job satisfaction, and improve the overall success of our institutions. In fact, some of the best administrators I've known weren't those who spent their days trying to implement big ideas. They were the ones who got the little details right and realized that small steps lead to great successes. In fact, you might say that the theme of this book is that if you take full advantage of each little moment that comes your way as an academic leader, the big issues will largely take care of themselves. Increasingly I've learned that small improvements are the best way to tackle big issues; sometimes they're the only way. To those who trot out the old objection that you can't cross a twelve-foot canyon in two six-foot jumps, I'd reply, "Of course. I couldn't agree with you more. But how many times in your travels have you ever *really* had to cross a twelve-foot canyon?"

- For readers who regard the typical book about academic administration as an invasive species that has somehow been transplanted from the world of business to the world of higher education, I'd like to provide a resource that's practical because it relates to what academic leaders really do. The suggestions in this book are all drawn from my own experience as a department chair, dean, and vice president for academic affairs, as well as dozens of workshops that I've conducted for university administrators all over the world. I'm certain that every reader will find some of the entries in this book more useful than others, but I'm equally sure that each person's list of the suggestions that really mattered to him or her will be different. For this reason, I've avoided offering ideas that may sound impressive but are ultimately impractical (the bane of most management books) and have tried to fill each day with advice that works.

- For those who know someone who has recently been appointed to an administrative position, this book would be a useful gift. You can include *Academic Leadership Day by Day* with a card of congratulations (or perhaps a

sympathy card) inscribed, "You're going to need this!" I
wish I'd received a book of this sort when my dean told me
that I was going to be my department's next chair—effective
immediately. I had no idea what my new job entailed. Every
other member of my department was only a year or two
from retirement, and I was the youngest member of the
faculty. My teaching load at that time included at least four
courses every semester, not to mention scholarship I needed
to complete if I ever wanted to be considered for promotion
and tenure. I simply didn't have time to read a library of
books on academic leadership and decide which of them was
useful. A guide that gave me one good idea a day would've
been perfect, so I've finally gotten around to creating one.
I hope it finds its way to all brand-new university chairs, not
to mention deans, provosts, and presidents.

• For faculty members or academic leaders who hope
to attain a higher position in administration within a year
or two, I wanted to write a book that would help you prepare for the application process and interviews. You'll find
in these daily entries a year-long coaching session that will
help you prepare for the types of questions you're likely to
be asked and for the level of experience you'll be expected
to have. If you follow the suggestions I have outlined in this
guide, you'll be a better administrator at the same time that
you amass the sort of expertise in budgetary management,
program review, institutional advancement, and other
activities that today's administrators today are expected
to master. You can think of this book as your daily administrative horoscope. But rather than offering you only vague

suggestions about things that may possibly occur in your personal life, *Academic Leadership Day by Day* will guide you to small but significant steps toward greater administrative effectiveness. You may already have considered many of these suggestions on your own, and several of the others may strike you as extremely easy, perhaps even somewhat trivial. But in order to keep each day's activity manageable within the schedule of an active administrator, I've focused on the small tasks we know we ought to be doing rather than the extravagant plans we'll probably never fulfill. My goal is to give you that extra voice of encouragement you'll sometimes need to take even a slight step toward making a big improvement in your program and perhaps also open the door to an exciting career opportunity in the future.

❖

If you're bothered by inconsistency, I should warn you now that *Academic Leadership Day by Day* encourages you to try one approach one day and then a few weeks later to do the precise opposite. For instance, you'll find advice in these pages to think as positively as you can only a few entries before I recommend that you practice a little self-doubt, instructions about not wasting time building something that others have already perfected only to be told a week or so later to go ahead and reinvent the wheel, encouragement to plan as carefully as you can rubbing shoulders with the advice to focus only on today, and so on. That contradiction is not accidental. No single approach works equally well for every administrator every day with every problem. By taking a few small steps to experiment with different approaches at different times, you'll end the academic year with an entire toolbox of ideas you can use as new opportunities arise and unanticipated challenges occur. You'll discover that you'll come away from this book with a better understanding of which tools work best for you and which don't fit your personal style or situation. You'll have a better sense of how to respond to difficult problems that no one ever told you were in your job description.

To switch metaphors for a moment, think of this book as something of an administrative buffet. You don't have to like every dish that's offered to you—you actually don't even have to sample them all—but you can pick and chose among the suggestions I've offered in order to find those that suit your taste, institution, and individual needs. There is so much variety in academic life today that some of these entries may not relate at all to what you do. One person may see the entry about sharing a meal with students in the dining hall and think, "What dining hall? We're an online university," while another person may think, "Which dining hall? We've got more than a dozen campuses." That sort of question will inevitably arise in a world where colleges and universities vary almost unimaginably in size, mission, delivery platforms, scope, and focus. Feel free, in other words, to pass by ideas that do not relate at all to your situation and to focus on those that you find truly appropriate to your unique position. I hope that by the end of the academic year, you'll have encountered more of the latter than the former.

Academic years begin on many different dates, and it's unlikely that yours will start precisely on September 1. But it didn't feel right to begin in the middle of a month, and there was no way to select the correct date for everyone's calendar every year anyway. So if the suggestions in this book don't begin until a week or two after your semester is already under way, consider that my gift to you: a few days of leisure at the start of a busy year. I'll get even with you anyway by continuing to offer suggestions for several days after graduation next spring. Oh, and one last word of advice: you don't have to wait until next September 1 to begin using this guide. Simply find today's date, dive in, and begin improving your program for your faculty, students, staff, and yourself. Have a terrific year!

❖

Jupiter, Florida   Jeffrey L. Buller
August 15, 2010

ACADEMIC LEADERSHIP DAY BY DAY

September

September 1

✧ *Take advantage of new beginnings.*

We're privileged in higher education to experience several beginnings each year. The beginning of the academic year brings new possibilities. So does the start of the calendar year. And so does the approach of a new term, though in a less dramatic way. All of these beginnings offer an incredible opportunity: we can let go of what wasn't successful in the past and rededicate ourselves to the potential of the future. We can be continually enriched by new students, new colleagues, and new ideas. So as the academic year gets under way today, spend a few moments looking for opportunities to take a fresh start at your approach to administration. If you've made decisions in the past that didn't work out as well as you'd hoped, release yourself from their burden. Don't lose track of the lessons you learned from them, but give yourself permission to let go of the guilt or disappointment that may still be attached to them. Make the year that's just begun the one in which you start making the sort of difference you've always hoped for. Continue today's reflection until you can identify some specific objective in your professional life that would be exciting to achieve and resolve that this is going to be the year in which you achieve that goal.

September 2

❖ *Know your limits.*

It's no secret that there are both things you can control and things that are beyond your control, and it's a wise person who knows how to tell the difference. Sometimes, however, academic administrators blur the line between the two because they're so eager to advance an idea that they waste valuable energy trying to transform things that are impervious to change. Like it or not, some people can't be brought onboard an endeavor no matter how persuasively you speak. Some budgetary situations are so dire that regardless of how painful they may be, major cuts will have to be made. Some potential donors are so committed to the causes they already support that it's impossible to interest them in a project with a different focus. And despite the best advice you give, there are certain things that you just can't make people do and certain people you can't encourage to do anything at all. With these limitations in mind, take a candid look at whatever in your environment or working life is beyond your control. Make a resolution that you'll let certain things go and stop frustrating yourself by continuing to devote useless energy to something you can't change. What will result is that you'll now have much more time, energy, and enthusiasm to spend on projects where you can make a positive difference.

September 3

❖ *Read the biography of an exemplary leader.*

As a way of contributing to your own professional development, select a biography of a leader you've always admired, and start reading it today. The leader you choose doesn't have to be a figure from higher education. It can be someone who demonstrated great leadership skills in the arts, government, business, the military, nonprofit organizations, religion, humanitarian causes, or any other branch of activity that interests you. As you read the book, try to identify specific values that enabled this leader to be successful and consider ways in which you could demonstrate those values in your own work. Whether we realize it or not, we're often attracted to heroes and role models who demonstrate the same qualities that others also see in us (although almost certainly at a different level). Be sure to notice, too, ways in which the leader you're reading about differs from you in some significant way—in the manner in which you would have approached a particular situation or a core principle that you hold dear, for example. The goal, after all, is to be inspired by a great leader's example, not to try to duplicate everything that he or she achieved or represented.

September 4

❖ *Attend a meeting just to listen.*

Effective academic leaders learn as much as possible about all the programs, committees, and people they supervise. As a way of growing in knowledge, ask to be invited to a meeting of a department, committee, or task force somewhere within your area of responsibility. Make it clear that your goal isn't to make a presentation or even to answer questions (unless those questions are particularly germane to the topics on the agenda), but simply to listen to the discussion as it unfolds. By sitting quietly and attending to others as they talk, you'll gain a better insight into the issues that different committees are grappling with right now—and you'll learn more about how they address those issues— than you would by reading through volumes of minutes and white papers. Remember, too, that your goal should not be to critique the operation of the committee, but simply to learn how things really work at your institution.

September 5

❖ *Review your program's publications.*

Take some time today to gather as many of your area's publications as you can. Don't forget that the term *publications* now includes electronic resources, such as Web sites and podcasts. Go through all of these resources and pretend that you're seeing them for the first time. Forget that you know anything at all about your institution and its programs so you can take a fresh look at the impression that these materials convey. Is there a consistency of image and message, or do the materials seem to convey conflicting impressions? If you were a potential student, donor, or faculty member, what about the style, content, and theme of these materials would make you eager to become involved in this program? You may come away from this activity with the sense that some of your materials need to be revised or replaced. But today's activity will be equally successful if you are satisfied with the publications you now have and develop greater appreciation for everyone whose work went into them.

September 6

❖ *Reorder your tasks.*

When students are having difficulty completing exams successfully, it can be beneficial to review with them the ways they approach questions during a test. Some students do better if they work consistently through an exam from beginning to end; if they try to skip around and do sections out of order, they easily become distracted and forget to complete certain questions. Other students do better by answering the easiest questions first; in this way, they build their confidence and are less likely to run out of time by devoting all of their energy to one or two particularly challenging questions. Still others perform best when they start with the hardest questions; by the end of the test period, their energy or ability to focus may be lapsing, making it harder for them to succeed at complex or challenging problems. In one way or another, all of us are like these students. Sometimes we're most productive when we work consistently through whatever comes our way. Sometimes we're more effective when we take on our greatest challenges early in the day when we have more stamina. And sometimes doing a series of easy tasks builds our energy and confidence, making thorny issues less daunting to tackle. With this revelation in mind, experiment today with reordering your tasks. Find out whether one of these approaches is more productive for you than the others and, if so, whether it is always more productive or only when you must deal with certain types of issues.

September 7

❖ *Be a coach.*

Coaches teach in ways that are different from the methods most instructors use. They hector, cajole, praise, flatter, motivate, intimidate, and challenge. Students often accept a far more scathing critique of their shortcomings from a coach than they would from a professor in one of their courses because of this different relationship. We expect coaches to set almost impossibly high expectations for us and to use whatever strategies they think are necessary to help us reach those expectations. Of course, not everything that a coach does involves badgering team members. Good coaches also convey a can-do attitude and help individuals achieve a higher degree of excellence than they ever thought possible. Coaches reinforce positive values even while they refuse to accept excuses or self-pity when things aren't going well. Today, consider how you might bring some of these coaching strategies to your responsibilities as an administrator. Who on your faculty and staff could benefit from some excellent coaching, not just to make the program better but to make that person better and more successful at what he or she does?

September 8

❖ *Waste time.*

The title of today's suggestion is, I must admit, intentionally misleading. Today's goal really isn't to waste time itself, but to become more aware of the ways in which you waste time. All of us have habits or practices that aren't as efficient as we might like them to be. Perhaps we hold on to responsibilities that could more productively be delegated to others. We may proofread our e-mails two or three times for minor typos when the recipient is unlikely to care about an occasional insignificant mistake. Or we may agonize over the phrasing of a memo that could have been written in next to no time if we had asked an administrative assistant to prepare an initial draft that we then polished and adapted to our own style. It's possible, too, that we may waste time working with a committee for months to develop a new policy or outline a new procedure that isn't measurably different from what we could have found already in place at dozens of other colleges and universities if we had performed a quick Internet search. Make it your goal today to be conscious of how you spend your time from moment to moment. Try to identify at least three to five practices that aren't your most productive uses of time. What could you accomplish for the benefit of your program if you hadn't wasted time on these inefficient activities but instead had directed your energy toward goals that made a more significant difference to your students and faculty members?

September 9

❖ *Learn from a bad decision.*

Not all of our administrative decisions end up being successful. There are always opportunities that we missed, mistakes that we made, or choices that we later came to regret. Spend a few minutes today identifying and reflecting on a truly bad professional decision. Engage in this exercise not to wallow in blame or attempt to rewrite history, but to learn something important from your error. Had you neglected to use important information that was available to you? Were you overly hasty or confident? Did you rely excessively on the advice of others? Use this reflection as a means of becoming a better administrator. Try to identify at least one thing you'll resolve to do differently in the future in order to avoid adding to the list of decisions you later regret.

September 10

❖ *Reflect on respect.*

Spend a few moments today considering how much respect other people seem to give you in your position and how much respect you believe you are giving others. Most administrators discover that the amount of trust they receive is almost directly proportionate to the amount they give the people around them. Sometimes academic leaders balk at this idea and say, in effect, "Presidents, deans, and professors shouldn't be the ones deferring to students. Respect has to be earned, and, like it or not, it can move in only one direction at a college or university." In some ways, that observation may be true. But respect isn't the same as obsequiousness. Respect is the way in which we demonstrate that other people have value, even if that value arises only from their potential. The president who doesn't show consideration for deans, the dean who disrespects faculty members, and the professor who is dismissive of students undermines his or her own authority. Evaluate yourself candidly today on the level of respect you're demonstrating to others. Then consider whether there seems to be any correlation between the amount of respect you show your colleagues and the amount you're shown in return.

September 11

❖ *Provide an outlet for dissent.*

Colleges and universities thrive on dissent. Students are regularly being challenged to examine accepted truths critically and to regard no answer as final. Professors spend years perfecting the art of examining the ideas of others, seeking contradictions or other types of logical flaws, and developing new perspectives. It's only inevitable that these practices will spill over from the study of an academic discipline to an examination of policies, procedures, and decisions that are made throughout higher education itself. For this reason, no matter how congenial your institution may be or how accomplished you have become as an academic leader, you are likely to encounter frequent, vigorous dissent. And that's a *good* thing. Dissent helps administrators keep their perspectives sharp and prevents institutions from falling into groupthink. Learning about opposing views before a final decision is announced can even help us avoid mistakes or ill-considered actions. So devote a few

12

minutes today to considering a new venue where people will be safe when they engage in constructive dissent. You could set aside a certain number of office hours every week or two when anyone who wishes can feel free to voice to you, without fear of retribution or condemnation, any view he or she wishes. You could establish an online threaded discussion where comments, suggestions, and opposing opinions can be expressed anonymously. You could survey your faculty, staff, and students to gain a better sense of their priorities. Each campus and each unit is likely to have its own preferred method for voicing dissent. But whatever it is, there are powerful and important voices out there that, one way or another, you need to hear.

September 12

⁘ *Tell your supervisor what you need.*

You've probably already encountered a student, faculty member, or member of the staff who got fairly far along into an activity—perhaps even past the deadline— and proved to be unsuccessful for a reason that you could easily have prevented. "Why didn't you just ask me for help?" you probably said, to which the response might have been, "But I didn't know I could!" or "I just wanted to figure it out on my own." A willingness to be independent can be an admirable quality. But chances are that when you heard the other person's answer, you felt frustrated and perhaps even spoke with the person about precisely what your role is and when it's permissible (even essential) to ask for help. Today, try to understand that your supervisor feels exactly this way. As administrators, we are sometimes reluctant to state our needs clearly and unambiguously to our bosses. We may think that it makes us look weak or give the impression that we're not up to the job. In fact, the reverse is true: effective leaders have enough self-confidence to tell their supervisors precisely what their needs are. You don't want to be like a student or employee who failed because of a misguided reluctance to ask for help. Make that call to your supervisor, and explain what you need right now in order to be most successful in your job.

September 13

·:· *Learn more about today's college students.*

All of us in higher education are tempted to try to recreate for others the best parts of our own college experience. We want others to have the same advantages that we did. But it's important to realize that college students today also want their own college experience, and that expectation may differ in crucial ways from what you valued most when you went to school. For instance, you may have found that campus life and vigorous discussions in the residence hall were truly life-changing experiences for you, while you now work in an environment where students prefer to live

at home. You may cherish your memories of those intellectually rich interactions over coffee with a favorite professor
but discover that most of the students around you prefer to
take their courses online. It's important, in other words,
to distinguish between the essence of what made your own
college experience so significant—an introduction to new
ways of viewing the world, intense and lasting relationships, a greater understanding of yourself and your role in
life—and specific ways of providing that experience. Spend
some time today learning about what's important to the
students in your program. What do they do in their free
time? What motivates them? How do they see the world?
By learning as much as you can about today's college students, you may find any number of ways to unite the best
of your own experiences with the needs and interests of a
different generation.

September 14

❖ *Convey some good news and some bad news.*

Academic leaders frequently commit one of two
opposing errors: they either focus too exclusively on their
own successes or become overly preoccupied with their
challenges, frustrations, and problems. You can see these
tendencies all around you. Sometimes administrators feel
the need to present the governing board, prospective
students, and other external stakeholders a picture of the

institution as though it easily progressed from one triumph to the next. Sometimes those same administrators confront other stakeholders, such as members of the faculty or staff, with endless tales of woe related to the budget, enrollment trends (where there are always either too many or too few students who want to attend the school), and issues of morale. The fact of the matter is that the news at any college or university is rarely, if ever, purely good or purely bad. The tendency to present that type of picture results from a desire to tell people what we think they want to hear, create a context that makes our own work easier, or both. Today, make a conscious effort to work against this destructive trend. You don't have to be so obvious as to indulge in the old cliché, "Well, I've got some good news and some bad news. . . ." But resolve to present a clear, complete, and accurate picture of both the successes and the challenges your program has experienced. You'll discover that doing so is not as difficult as you may believe and that in the long run it improves your credibility immeasurably.

September 15

❖ *Describe your supervisor.*

What immediately comes to mind when you think of the person or board to whom you report? What positive qualities can you identify? What negative impressions do you have? Are there descriptive terms that are neither particularly positive nor negative that help define who your boss is? Do you find that you resent or fear this person? Do you sometimes feel that you could do your supervisor's job better than he or she does? Consider the description that you develop today, and then identify specific experiences that led you to those impressions. Reflect, too, on whether you believe that you may be demonstrating to your supervisor how you feel through your actions, expressions, or word choice. Particularly if your impressions are more negative than positive, are there ways in which you are causing potential harm to yourself by the attitude that you are conveying, even subconsciously? Once this exercise is complete, delete or shred your list of descriptive terms. After all, you don't want anyone else to see what you've written.

September 16

❖ *Stop—at least for a moment.*

Administrators sometimes believe that they have to be doing something all the time. If they're not active—not changing things for the better—they often feel that they're not doing their jobs. But today, take at least a moment or two—and just stop. Reflect on all the good that's occurring in your program. Appreciate the people with whom you work. Take pride in what you've already accomplished, and feel gratitude for the accomplishments of others. Pause long enough that you no longer feel you're doing one thing solely to get to the next thing but are really experiencing the full benefit of all the wonderful success around you.

Then carry some of that positive energy with you throughout the rest of your day.

September 17

⁓ *Remember that it's not all about you.*

Spend today trying not merely to *see* things from the perspective of your colleagues, but actually to understand how it *feels* in their world. Who works with you and is facing some challenges? The young faculty member who's uncertain about the prospects for promotion or tenure? The colleague who's undergoing a difficult divorce? The long-term employee who feels that everything at the school was better twenty or thirty years ago? The person who's trying to make ends meet or facing a medical emergency? The parent whose children have special needs? Every member of your local cast of characters has his or her own particular problems, worries, individual interests, and hopes for the future. It can be easy when people seem irritated or aloof to ask yourself, "What have I done to deserve *that* reaction?" But make it a point today to remember that it's not always about you. In fact, it's frequently not about you. People tend to respond to situations because of where they are in their lives right now. If it's in your power to do so, try helping them with their challenges, but even when you're unable to help, try to view the issue as objectively as possible.

September 18

❖ *Share someone else's dream.*

Ask someone who reports to you to tell you about his or her greatest hope for the future. That hope might be a personal ambition, a vision for your program or school, or even a dream that's far more global. But even if the idea that's presented to you today is wholly impractical or doesn't appeal to you at all, don't judge it. Just listen and try to understand what motivates this colleague. If you can, appreciate the vision that he or she has for the future. Thank your colleague for sharing a vision with you that may be extremely private and may never have been shared with anyone else before. And then consider your own dream and how you would answer a question about what you hoped for most in all the world.

September 19

❖ *Learn from what others teach.*

Gather at least five to ten syllabi from courses being taught in your area and examine them. Your goal isn't to catch a faculty member in violation of this or that policy, and it's certainly not to criticize the courses themselves or suggest better ways of organizing them. Rather, the goal of this exercise is to develop a better sense of how others teach the material in their disciplines, what they regard as particularly important, and why they've structured the course as they did. Some disciplines, particularly at the introductory level, have a fairly standard way of approaching topics, and you're unlikely to find much variation even at institutions very different from your own. But in other fields and at upper levels of nearly every discipline, professors often have a lot more liberty to group topics in innovative ways, tackle certain issues first while saving others for near the end of the course, and place an individual stamp on the way in which they teach the material. Do you see the personalities of your colleagues in how they write their syllabi? Do you find any surprises—maybe delightfully creative ways of organizing a course that you would never have thought of on your own? Are there references to assignments that seem particularly inventive? Try to come away from your review with a new appreciation for how well professors teach in the area that you supervise and a renewed enthusiasm for the instructional mission of your college or university.

September 20

❖ *Evaluate without making value judgments.*

Administrators frequently have to evaluate ideas, requests, and people. There are times too when you'll need to instruct someone to do something in a particular way because of institutional procedures, style guidelines, or your supervisor's preferences. It can be difficult to convey the message, "I need you to do this differently," without appearing as if you are saying, "You are doing this wrong!" or even, "You're incompetent at what you're doing!" But effective administrators have to make that distinction very clear. So today, whenever you must evaluate someone or change his or her behavior in some way, seek ways of doing so without making the person feel unappreciated, disrespected, or demeaned. Try to accomplish this task even if today's the day you must conduct the appraisal of a professor whose students never seem to grasp even the most rudimentary material, who has no prospects in sight for any productive scholarship, and who refuses to take on even the lightest committee load. None of these problems make the faculty member you're reviewing a bad person, although you may have some suggestions about how he or she might better meet the school's expectations of its employees. The goal, in other words, is to evaluate people without making value judgments about them, to help them improve their performance without degrading them as individuals. This goal should be one that you pursue every day, but make it a special priority today.

September 21

❖ *Be the change you want to see.*

One of Mahatma Gandhi's most commonly quoted sayings is his encouragement to "be the change you want to see in the world." Accomplishing that lofty goal may seem a bit overwhelming as a task to take on during a single day in your life as an administrator, but today at least, try to be the change you want to see in your own world. In other words, if you work in an environment that's torn apart by mistrust and conflict, spend today extending trust and understanding to everyone you meet. If your program suffers from lack of direction or energy, be focused in all of your duties, and bring vigor to everything that comes your way. Whatever it is that you feel needs to occur in your environment, reflect that in your own attitude and interactions with others. If there's anything that, in your opinion, exists too abundantly in the program that you supervise (such as too much criticism, prolonged deliberation, or personal work done on office time), diminish that behavior, quality, or attitude in the way you think, talk, and act. Certainly you won't be able to effect a significant or lasting change in a single day, but you may discover a path to begin taking in the direction that your program or institution needs to go.

September 22

❖ *Respect other people's time.*

Sometimes the best thing an academic leader can do is to cancel a meeting when it's clear that the agenda isn't important enough to occupy anyone's time. Everyone's busy, and a good academic leader doesn't occupy more of someone else's schedule than is necessary. Every day we come across plenty of ways to help leverage the limited time that people have in their schedules. For instance, you could review the work assignments of everyone who reports to you in order to make sure that the right tasks are assigned to the right people; updated job descriptions can help everyone become engaged and properly challenged, and neither overwhelmed nor bored. In addition, you could check to make sure that everyone knows precisely what's expected in his or her responsibilities, what acceptable standards of achievement are, and when upcoming deadlines will occur. A person who doesn't know your expectations is likely to waste time doing things wrong, which then causes even more time to be spent doing the task the right way. You can also help people prioritize their tasks, so that urgent day-to-day business doesn't crowd out more important long-term goals, resulting in a lot of fires that have been put out but almost nothing of lasting significance that's been achieved. You can work with people to incorporate their own dreams into their assignments so that what helps them also helps the institution, and vice versa. Effective administrators are continually looking for ways to respect the time of the faculty and staff members who help make their program a success. Find at least one of these ways today.

September 23

❖ *Consider the first thing you do at work every day.*

What's the first thing you do when you come to work every day? As soon as you answer this question, consider what your answer reveals about your values and priorities. There's no right or wrong answer to this question (unless, of course, you said that the very first thing you do is to pick up your copy of *Academic Leadership Day by Day* and check that day's activity, in which case all I can say is, "Bravo!"), merely different ways of learning about your administrative style. For instance, if you spend a significant amount of time greeting your coworkers and finding out what's new in their lives, that beginning of your day shows the importance that you place on networking and social relationships. If the first thing you do is check your e-mail, your highest priority appears to be the processing of information. If your initial impulse is to examine your calendar and establish a few clear priorities for the day, you probably place a premium on organization and planning. So your goal today is not only to identify *what* you tend to do first each day, but also *why*. Make sure your first task clearly reflects what you want your priorities to be, and be particularly concerned if you realize that your time tends to get occupied from the very start of your day with unproductive or inessential matters. If that's what occurs, see if you can start reprogramming your day so that your first task makes a positive difference to the mission of your college or university.

September 24

❖ *Find the weakest link.*

Even the strongest chain has its weakest link. You may be fortunate enough to have a faculty in which every member is a spectacular instructor. Even so, one of them is likely to be marginally less spectacular than the others. Everybody on your staff may be dedicated, exceptionally hard working, and personable, but surely one of them doesn't quite reach the lofty heights of all the rest. The goal of identifying your weakest link isn't to be punitive; it's to determine what your best strategy should be in order to help this person become even better. Sometimes weak links need better training, stronger encouragement, or closer supervision. Sometimes their assignments need to be changed so that they can devote more of their time to what they do best. Only occasionally will you discover such a poor fit between what a job requires and what the employee can do that a complete reassignment or dismissal is necessary. Even then, what you're really doing is freeing the person to pursue other possibilities in which he or she is likely to have greater success. So view today's goal of identifying your weakest link not as a way of finding out who's "failing" at his or her job, but as your chance to help each person who reports to you do his or her work even better. After all, someday your own supervisor may also be looking for his or her own weakest link.

September 25

❖ *Go back to the future.*

There are many ways of dealing with the future. You can fantasize about what you hope will occur, dread what you fear might occur, and think about what you believe is likely to occur. Today, pursue the last of these approaches. Being neither particularly optimistic nor pessimistic about the future, where do you reasonably expect to see yourself ten years from today? If you think that you'll be in your same position, what will you have accomplished during that time? If you're going to be in a different position or working somewhere else, what steps took you there? If you will have retired, what did you do in order to secure your financial future and establish a legacy of your career? Be as practical as you can in imagining what the world will be like and what your role will be. Extrapolate from where you are right now, and see if you can identify the trends that are likely to shape the next decade. Are there ways in which you can do things today in order to improve your probable future?

September 26

❖ *Lead by serving.*

Service consists of all the things we do for the benefit of others. If we lead to help those around us, not in order to secure own self-interest or advance our personal success, then we lead by serving. The effectiveness we have in our positions can often increase when we change the way in which we view what we're trying to achieve. Today, make a conscious effort to approach every decision, appointment, meeting, and other responsibility by asking, "How are my actions here helping others to the greatest extent possible?" You may find that your whole approach to today's challenges will change. You'll regard unexpected problems not as distractions from your "real work," but as the substance of your real work: an opportunity to make one more difference in the lives of others.

September 27

❖ *Simplify something.*

Colleges and universities are complex, and they tend to develop policies, procedures, and strategies that are similarly complex. Because colleges and universities tend to be long-lived, those policies, procedures, and strategies often become even more byzantine over time. In many cases, however, that degree of complexity is neither necessary nor desirable. Try to find a situation today in which a welcome degree of simplification is possible in the area you supervise. There must be some committee structure, approval procedure, or review mechanism that originally served a perfectly good purpose but now gets in your way or prevents progress. Streamline and pare things down in order to make them more efficient and less burdensome to the people who use them. Come away from this activity with the clear understanding that improving academic policies and procedures doesn't always mean adding something new. It can also mean clearing away obstructions and debris, leaving something behind that is simpler but more elegant.

September 28

❖ *Study interactions.*

An almost unbelievable amount of higher education administration depends on good interpersonal communication skills. Although searches for academic leaders frequently focus on our knowledge of strategic planning, resource development, and leadership in such areas as research, curriculum planning, and assessment, it's in interpersonal relationships that we have to direct most of our efforts. Tensions arise, conflicts break out, and employees become disengaged. We're constantly trying to inspire, motivate, cajole, or dissuade others from ill-advised pursuits, and relatively few of us have sufficient training in handling interpersonal relationships. For this reason, make it a point today to learn something new about interpersonal communication and how it affects the people in your area. The course of action you decide to follow could range anywhere from registering for a workshop on effective ways to interact with people to learning five effective strategies to calm others down when they're angry. No matter what you learn today, it's sure to become extremely useful soon, working as we all do in environments with short deadlines, large egos, and increasing pressure.

September 29

❖ *Seek your own satisfaction.*

While effective academic leaders are primarily motivated by their ability to help others, it's also important for them to find some satisfaction in their jobs. An administrator who's simply going through the motions or resents much of what he or she is doing is unlikely to be serving the best interests of the program. Today, be sure to identify at least one way you can increase your own job satisfaction. Then go out and do it. Although this suggestion may seem a bit self-centered, it's impossible to give others what you don't have yourself. If there's a project that has long been annoying or distressing you, see if someone else can complete it—or maybe it doesn't need to be completed at all. Explore whether there's a better way to achieve the same goal. If you find yourself exasperated by the constant demands of work, see if you can schedule one three-day weekend a month, giving yourself an oasis of time to look forward to in the midst of unreasonably tight deadlines and ceaseless pressure. Ask yourself, "If I could change one thing that would increase my job satisfaction, what would it be?" Then give yourself the freedom to pursue it.

September 30

❖ *Read a boring book.*

Despite the common injunction not to judge a book by its cover, we actually do exactly that all the time. No one could possibly read all the books that are written or even have time for all those that intrigue us, so we glance at the artwork on the front when we're browsing for something to read, look at the brief descriptions that appear on the dust covers, and make an educated guess as to whether the book will be worth our time to read it. Sometimes we're absolutely correct, but frequently we're disappointed. We hardly ever read a book (unless we're required to do so for some reason) if we think it's going to be boring, annoying, or unrelated to our interests. Yet today's activity is to do exactly that. Find a book about some topic that doesn't appeal to you at all. In fact, the greater your aversion to the topic, the better your experience is going to be. As you read the book, it's likely that you won't change your overall opinion of the subject matter, but at least you'll come away from this experience better educated about something you may not otherwise have learned about in any depth. As Pliny the Elder said, no book is so bad that you can't get *something* good out of it. You may also find that the topic you had assumed was so dull and uninviting is actually more interesting than you ever would have known if you hadn't taken this opportunity to read about it. The best academic administrators don't remain satisfied with knowing about only the topics they've already mastered. They're always seeking to expand their insights.

October

October 1

❖ *Take stock.*

The beginning of October is a particularly interesting time at most colleges and universities. According to the calendar, we're in the last quarter of the year, and that makes it a good time to look back on the progress we've made and consider the further plans we need to develop. But at the vast majority of schools that follow the North American academic calendar, the school year has been under way for only a little over a month, so there's still plenty of time for ambitious goals to be achieved and long-term projects to be completed. For this reason, spend some time today taking stock of your progress. Where are you right now in terms of the work you're doing in achieving your highest priorities? What are the greatest challenges you're facing? What will disappoint you the most if it isn't completed or achieved before the end of the academic year? Are there any objectives you're hoping to complete this semester that could benefit from a little extra effort right now? Taking stock of precisely where you are today in terms of your goals will help prevent you from getting to the end of either the calendar or academic year without accomplishing at least part of what you've decided is most important for yourself and your institution.

October 2

❖ *Ask questions.*

There's a scene in Tom Stoppard's *Rosencrantz and Guildenstern Are Dead* in which the title characters participate in a game that's usually known as Questions. In this game, each participant replies to every question with another question that makes sense in the context. That question is expected to lead to still another question, and so forth. If a player makes a statement, issues a command, or utters an exclamation, that person drops out, and the other participants continue. While you probably don't want to play this game in everything you do, today's suggestion is to approach everything that comes your way for the next twenty-four hours with a questioning attitude. In other words, ask *lots* of questions. Question assumptions, and follow up each new revelation with still more questions. The goal isn't to engage in this activity in an accusatorial manner or in a way that wastes people's time. Seek to understand rather than to annoy. Question past practices in order to make sure that decisions aren't being made simply because "we've always done it that way." Question arguments in order to verify the strength of people's reasoning. Question everyone around you to understand how they solve problems and handle responsibility. If you let this practice get out of hand, you'll find that people start treating you like the child who asks, "Why?" after every answer he or she is given. But if you conduct this experiment thoughtfully, you may just hit on the very question that leads to more effective, creative, and productive ways of accomplishing something important.

October 3

❖ *Exhibit candor.*

One of the lessons that nearly all academic leaders learn—some almost immediately, others only after long years of struggle—is that it's extremely important to be as open and transparent in your administrative style as possible. Certainly there are aspects of our work for which a high degree of confidentiality is essential. Student grades and health information, many personnel processes, and records containing Social Security numbers or account passwords all fall into the category of materials that need to be guarded carefully. But much more of what an administrator does not only can but should be shared widely with the community. Rumors begin, and anxiety levels increase when people work in an environment where they believe that important discussions are being made in secret. If an administrator doesn't indicate that a certain action is at least possible or under consideration, a belief that something far worse is going to happen will soon arise. People assume that a lack of candor means that unpleasant truths are being withheld. For this reason, scrutinize all your actions today to make certain that you are being as open as possible in as many situations as possible. Although there may well be some initial resistance to particular ideas or proposals, your increasing demonstration of candor could soon become an essential part of your administrative style.

October 4

❖ *Remove one obstacle.*

Everyone around you is trying to improve the quality of education and research at your school, each in his or her own way. Some of your colleagues pursue this goal in grand, perhaps even spectacular, ways. Others make a series of smaller contributions, all of them important to the mission of your school. Today, make your own modest contribution to these efforts by doing whatever is necessary to remove one small obstacle to someone else's progress. You might make an introduction to an important contact on someone's behalf, waive a requirement that is preventing a task from being completed, or provide a small amount of seed money to test an idea. Like the improvements that are occurring all around you, the obstacle that you remove today doesn't have to be very large (although think how wonderful the result would be if it were); it just has to lead to progress. If you complete today's task successfully, you'll know exactly how to answer yourself later in the day when you ask, "Now what did I do today that was of any significance?"

October 5

❖ *Look around you.*

When we work in the same space day after day, we often stop paying attention to our environment. We're unaware of the impressions our workspace may have on those who are viewing it for the first time. We excuse disorder, justifying it on the grounds that that we've got a lot going on. (In actuality, we're deceiving ourselves. The mess in our offices is an indication that we're less organized and effective than we could be.) We believe that the sports memorabilia on our walls demonstrate our fervent loyalty to our favorite athletic teams and give our offices a sense of high energy. (They don't. They're more likely to alienate fans of other teams and give the impression that we've never grown up.) Because we can be blind to the impressions that others may have of the environment we work in, make an effort to see your office or desk today through new eyes. Will it strike someone as a place of energizing light or as blinding because of its excessive intensity? Will others regard it as subdued and relaxing or as dark and gloomy? Do the objects in your office make your workspace seem more personal or more cluttered? Does it appear that you're using desktops, shelves, and even the floor for storage of documents that really belong elsewhere? If someone doesn't know you at all, what conclusions would that person draw if he or she saw only your office?

October 6

❖ *Have confidence.*

No matter how much experience academic administrators may have, there are always times when they feel frustrated or insecure. They may be facing a situation they've never encountered before or dealing with opposition on a number of fronts simultaneously. The next time this happens to you, keep in mind that you're not really alone, although it may feel that way at the time. All of us who work in higher education administration have been in this situation, and it's an experience we're all likely to face repeatedly. But there's actually no problem that you can't handle. Many issues that feel impossibly challenging when they arise will later make you wonder why you were so disturbed by them. Remember that not every problem is a crisis. Your work now is to handle situations like this one, and you wouldn't have been trusted with your responsibilities if people didn't believe you were capable of coping with challenges. So approach everything you do today with confidence, and devote your effort to solving the problems that come along, not to second-guessing yourself.

October 7

❖ *Attend a campus event.*

There are many satisfying reasons for attending campus events, even if it means going back to campus on an evening when you'd rather stay at home and relax. First, these opportunities allow you to sample a broader range of what your college or university has to offer. Even if you've been to many campus events before, it's important to be reminded regularly that it is through these activities that students and campus visitors see the institution and develop their opinions about it. Second, campus events provide us with insight into how our institutions improve people's lives. Unless you go only to events you know you already enjoy, you'll find yourself learning about disciplines and recreational opportunities that you may encounter only rarely. And you may begin meeting people—including potential supporters of your own program—whose paths you wouldn't otherwise have crossed. Finally, being seen at these events allows members of the campus community to get to know you in ways different from how they see you in your professional capacity. Those broader relationships can help you become more effective as an administrator, even as your broader participation in campus events demonstrates that you're a good citizen of the entire college or university community.

October 8

❖ *See people, not tasks, as your first priority.*

It can be easy for academic leaders to become overly enamored of their to-do lists. Crossing off one achievement after another can give us a great feeling of achievement and make us believe that we're making significant progress. But it's important to remember that all of those tasks get placed on to-do lists as a means of helping others, not as ends in themselves. The true academic leader should never be too busy to be polite to faculty, students, and members of the staff. There will always be times when your calendar and list of goals will need to be abandoned so that you can assist someone with a problem or comfort someone in distress. Those personal interactions are a key component of your job. Even if they never appear on your personal to-do list or résumé, these opportunities to serve should always remain your highest priority.

October 9

❖ *Nominate someone for an award.*

Academic leaders are judged not so much for what they achieve themselves, but on the basis of what those they supervise achieve. The placement of your graduating students into highly prestigious postbaccalaureate programs or jobs, the publications and grants that faculty members receive, the accomplishments and further careers of your graduate students, the recognitions bestowed on your staff: all of these achievements are indications that you've succeeded as an academic leader. You can, of course, wait for others to notice the excellence of your programs. But almost everyone is preoccupied with his or her own work, so it can be useful to help this process along. Therefore, spend some time today identifying a person who has a clear chance of receiving an award and begin the nomination process that will lead to this honor. The award you target could be something specific to your own college or university, or it could be a major national or international recognition. By taking the initiative to nominate someone for this distinction, you are making an important contribution toward improving morale in your area, building value in your stakeholders, and drawing positive attention to your program or institution.

October 10

⁘ *Discover new ways to manage stress.*

There is no way of avoiding the fact that administrative positions can be highly stressful. So take some time today to learn a few effective ways of handling the pressure that comes with your job. Explore the Internet or browse through books and articles that deal with stress management. Perhaps you always wanted to know more about meditation, tai chi, or visualization techniques but never took the time to explore these topics. Perhaps a physical activity, such as running or working with a personal trainer, might help you reduce stress. Or there may be some emotional issues related to your family life that complicate the pressures you encounter at work but you've never explored the ways in which a counselor or social worker could help you cope with these challenges. Regardless of the type of stress you face or your individual situation, make it a priority today to learn at least one significant way to help you manage stress and thus be more effective in your day-to-day responsibilities.

October 11

❖ *Move on.*

As you'll see repeatedly in this guide, effective administration often requires perseverance. But sometimes effective administration also means cutting your losses. The important thing is to know the difference. Today's exercise is to build your insight in this area. Choose one goal, project, plan, commitment, or activity that hasn't been worth the effort that you and others have invested in it. Maybe it was a bad idea from the start, or maybe the situation has changed since you became involved. In either case, today's the day to let it go and move on. Don't linger over guilt or regret. Don't waste your time being annoyed that those who opposed the idea have somehow "won." Focus exclusively on the present moment, and consider what you'll be able to do with the time you're freeing up by abandoning this effort. Get something else done now, and recommit to a different project that will be far better served by your perseverance.

October 12

❖ *Assess your telephone style.*

A week ago you were encouraged to look around your office and see if you could determine what your workspace tells others about your personality, habits, and priorities. Today's suggestion is to do something similar with regard to your telephone style. We all convey a lot more than just information on the phone. We provide hints about how interested we are in the other caller, whether we regard his or her issue as important, what our management style is like, and whether we consider courtesy, service, and accessibility to be important. Most academic leaders seek a balance on the phone that allows them to be friendly but concise. They neither cause the other person to feel rushed nor do they allow a single call to monopolize too much time. And they never, ever multitask on the phone. As you make and receive several calls today, pay close attention to how you're probably coming across to the other person. Does your style change depending on whether you're talking to a superior, a colleague, someone who reports to you, an external constituent, or a student? What judgments are all of these people probably making about you on the basis of how you interact with them on the telephone?

October 13

❖ *Learn from a case study.*

Case studies are one of the best methods for administrators to improve their knowledge of key issues and their skills in making difficult decisions. A number of books of administrative case studies are available, others may be found online, and some professional organizations regularly include a case study session at their annual meetings. The method consists of analyzing short narratives based on actual situations or created out of fictitious but plausible circumstances that might arise at a college or university. A good case study doesn't suggest any single clear-cut solution; in fact, there is no right or wrong answer. Different approaches might be taken depending on the administrator's personal style, the nature of the institution, and numerous other factors that arise only when the case is examined in depth. As today's activity, try to locate a challenging case study based on the type of position you currently hold and the issues that you are most likely to face. As you work through the case study, analyze not merely the problem itself but also your individual approach to it. Do you think you would try to act alone so as to intervene quickly, or would you seek a consensus solution even though that might take much longer? Is the case about an emergency situation? If so, which offices on campus need to be alerted or involved? Are there approaches to the problem that might be effective in the short term but could lead to more challenging problems in the future? Do you find yourself attacking the challenge in a systematic and logical way, or do you have an initial, almost visceral impulse about the best method to be used?

October 14

❖ *Practice self-doubt.*

Many principles of modern education are based on the idea that before people can learn effectively, we must first build their self-esteem. People with low self-esteem frequently can't accomplish everything they hope for because their lack of confidence undermines their efforts. Professors too have long noted that whenever they tell a class of students that they're all brilliant and will learn the material easily, they frequently do. And when a class is told that a topic is extremely hard—particularly when the implication is that it will be too hard *for them*—they tend to underperform. It's undeniable that self-esteem and self-confidence are wonderful assets, but too much of them can be highly detrimental to good academic administration. If you're so confident in your judgments that you think you're incapable of making a mistake, you could be laying the groundwork for a major problem. While good academic leaders are never plagued with self-doubt, they sometimes use self-doubt as a tool. They challenge their decisions and their solutions, not so much as to become immobilized through uncertainty but enough to understand all sides of an issue. By practicing self-doubt, we don't destroy our confidence but we do make it far less likely that we'll fall prey to over-confidence, inflexibility, and complacency. As one tool among many, a little bit of self-doubt every now and then can help you become an even better academic leader.

October 15

⊰⊱ *Speak to a chronic latecomer.*

Every unit in every institution has them: the people who are never on time for a meeting or appointment. Sometimes they seem blissfully unaware of the inconvenience that their chronic lateness creates for everyone. Sometimes they seem to take a perverse sort of pleasure in suggesting that they are just much busier than everyone else and can't possibly meet all of their commitments on time. The problem with chronic latecomers is that they frequently waste other people's time when meetings or appointments can't start promptly or they have to be filled in on what occurred before they managed to arrive. In the worst cases, chronic latecomers can miss key information that was shared in their absence, resulting in harm for their students, their grant proposals, and their colleagues. Today, identify one chronic latecomer who reports to you, and talk to this person about the difficulties he or she is creating. If the person tries to justify this tardiness by saying that he or she is "just too busy," reply by asking what part of the job that person simply isn't up to or whether you need to find someone else who can handle those responsibilities better. The fact of the matter, you might remind the latecomer, is that we're *all* busy, and there's rarely a correlation between how frenzied or late a person is and how much work the person does or the quality of his or her achievements. Many chronic latecomers will not change their ways, but they can be put on notice about the problems they are causing others.

October 16

❖ *Put agendas on your agenda.*

Academic administrators make use of agendas so often that they hardly give them a second thought. There are written agendas, unwritten agendas, and that bane of every college or university: hidden agendas. Some committees seem to rely on the same agenda at every meeting. Other groups deal with so many types of issues that if there is not a detailed agenda, knowing what's going to happen at any particular meeting is all but impossible. Take some time today to review how you develop agendas for the meetings that you chair. Do you write them out and distribute them to all members at least a few days before the meeting takes place? If not, how do you expect the participants to come to the meeting fully prepared to discuss the issues that will be addressed and with all the documentation they might want to share with others? Do your agendas state both the beginning and ending times for the meeting? If they don't, do your meetings frequently drag on longer than they should or prove less productive than you might like? Do you carefully outline the topics for discussion and specify what actions need to be taken or decisions made? If you don't, do you find participants at your meetings straying from the most important topics, forgetting to follow up on important items, or returning to the same topics over and over? Consider today how well-designed agendas can help you conduct meetings that are more pleasant, productive, and focused. Be brutal when you need to be, and pare your meetings down to the essentials. Remember that the purpose of a meeting is not simply to meet, but to accomplish something significant.

October 17

❖ *Recommend a good book.*

We learn a lot about people from the books they read. When you're at a friend's house or in a faculty member's office and survey the books on the shelves, you probably gain some insight into that person's interests, perhaps even learn a few things about his or her personality. The books we enjoy say something important about us, even as we ourselves are changed and develop because of the books we read. With this idea in mind, talk with someone today about a book that's made a real difference in your life. Try to express not merely *that* you enjoyed the book, but *why* it resonated with you so much. Your conversation may then prompt the other person to recommend a good book. At the very least, you may receive a good suggestion for your own future reading. Even better, you may learn about an entirely new dimension in the character of one of your coworkers that helps transform your relationship. But the best thing you can achieve in your discussion with others of your favorite books is sharing with your colleagues a more complete understanding of who you are—and maybe also learning a thing or two about yourself in the process.

October 18

❖ *Raise awareness.*

Today's activity is to identify some way in which to help your local community raise its awareness of the important contributions your programs make. Perhaps a major speaker is coming to campus, and the information about his or her presentation could be included in the community calendar section of the local media. Perhaps one of your graduates has accomplished something significant that could provide the basis for a press release distributed by your institution's public relations office. Perhaps you could offer to speak at a meeting of a local service organization such as the Kiwanis or Rotary Club and bring positive attention to your program and institution. What you decide to do will depend a great deal on your own personality and the nature of the programs you supervise. But whatever you decide, follow through on this plan quickly in order to remind people in your local area about the contribution you, your faculty, and the students in your programs make to the lives of those who live in your community. Even if you're convinced that people already know about all the wonderful advantages that arise from having your institution in their community, you'll find it useful to provide this type of reminder on a regular basis.

October 19

❖ *Plot an escape.*

It's important in academic life to have a chance every now and then to pull back, recharge your batteries, and view your priorities in a more relaxed manner. Originally doing exactly that is what the idea of an academic sabbatical was intended to be: a year-long "sabbath" every seven years or so to read, reflect, and then return to daily responsibilities with renewed energy. Unfortunately, as a result of a well-intentioned desire to be fully accountable for the "productivity" of all its employees, many institutions have replaced these leisurely, unstructured sabbaticals with academic leaves for which faculty members must compete, identifying the "practical products" that will result from their "reassigned time." Applicants for sabbaticals thus prepare detailed proposals that outline exactly what they hope to achieve and expect to accomplish during their time away from their usual work, transforming what was once thought of as a period of reduced stress into a stressful, highly intense year of deadlines and goals. Take your own stand against this trend today. Spend a few moments luxuriating in the prospect of an extended period in which you'd be able to do exactly what you'd like. Suppose you had a year-long sabbatical or leave of absence with absolutely no strings attached. How would you spend your time? Why would those activities be important to you? Is there any way that you can incorporate some of them into your schedule even now, as busy as you are?

October 20

❖ *Be unique.*

What is it that you, and you alone, bring to your job? Regardless of the way in which others may think of our official duties, each of us redefines our positions in light of our own interests and personality. As a result, another person wouldn't approach your work in exactly the same way you do. So how would you characterize your personal and unique contribution to your job? What is the value you add to your college or university? You might start this thought experiment by identifying the most important task you do that's not included among your official list of duties, such as greeting new students as they move into the residence hall or introducing advanced students to distinguished scholars in your field. Think too about the personal traits that you bring to your position. By focusing today on what makes you unique as an academic leader, you'll be better able to describe to others how your program or institution has benefited from your service. (That insight can be extremely useful when it comes time to write your annual report.) You may also discover an area or two where you could benefit from using the talents of others in order to compensate for your own challenges or weakness.

October 21

❖ *Show someone you care.*

There are many misconceptions about academic leaders. Movies and television shows frequently depict college administrators as bungling incompetents or narrow-minded bureaucrats who stand in the way of youth and genius. But in fact, most chairs, deans, and senior administrators care quite deeply about students, faculty members, and the overall importance of higher education. Today, make it clear to a faculty member at your college or university that you care sincerely, not just about academic achievement in general, but about that person's teaching, learning, or research. Illustrate that you've taken the time to discover what's important to that professor and that you value the work he or she is doing. Remember that today's goal isn't to feign an interest or concern that you don't really have but rather to demonstrate the amount of involvement you have every day in the contributions people in your area make.

October 22

❖ *Question an assumption.*

Since it's impossible to have enough proof to confirm absolutely everything we believe, much of what we do in life must be based on our assumptions. For instance, we assume that students will learn best in a particular way, that certain preconditions are essential for a proper research environment, that people prefer to live and work in a place where specific rules are in place, and so on. Today, see if you can identify five or more of your own basic assumptions, and then proceed to question at least one of them. You might begin seeing if you can find studies and other sources of data that provide evidence either confirming or disproving what you've assumed. ("What real evidence is there that smaller class size leads to improved student learning?" "Have there been any studies to prove whether professors who are highly active in research tend also to be more effective teachers?" "Who has examined the correlation between participation in a living-learning community and the likelihood of graduating within four years?") Or you could challenge a basic assumption by considering the implications of an alternative point of view. ("Is it possible that morale would actually improve if we adopted a system of flat-rate increases rather than allocating merit pay?" "Would scheduling courses become a nightmare if faculty members were simply to select their own class times?" "Would our curriculum be significantly weakened if we decreased the number of required courses?") Questioning assumptions in this way may not always lead you to change your mind, but it will help you understand the line of reasoning that leads to your conclusions.

October 23

❧ *Define leadership.*

When you are demonstrating leadership in your position, what exactly is it that you're doing? How, in other words, do you define leadership? In your view, is leadership something a person is born with, or can anyone become effective as a leader? How is leadership similar to and different from such concepts as power, authority, and management? Having the differences among these concepts clearly in mind helps administrators understand better how to respond to various situations and how to advance the goals of their college or university. Try to think of these concepts in terms of whether the person is a leader because he or she is in control or because he or she empowers others. Consider, too, whether the leaders are ultimately trying to benefit themselves, the institution, specific stakeholders of the institution, society as a whole, or something else. Then think of the type of relationship that an academic leader develops with others and how that relationship might differ from that which people develop with a commanding officer, traditional boss, parent, manager, or coach. If none of these areas adequately captures what you believe is the essence of genuine leadership, try expressing your own ideas in a sentence or two, and then review your actions throughout the day to determine how well you live up to the values that you've described.

October 24

❖ *Stay on message.*

Although the duties of an academic administrator can change considerably from day to day—and frequently even during the course of a single day—consistency offers many benefits. When you give a speech or make a proposal about some issue, a single statement that a goal is important has far less effect than when people hear you address that same issue meeting after meeting. Staying on message helps you to convey to others that this issue is yours. You own it since it consistently motivates you as you make decisions. You may feel like a broken record at times, fearing that you'll be perceived as too insular or boring. But coming to be identified with a topic allows you to focus your energy and to achieve greater things as a result. Of course, today's suggestion isn't an activity that you can accomplish during a single day, but you can get this process under way. You can identify the topic that will be your most important message in the weeks and months to come. You can plan ways of gradually imbuing your remarks with references to this idea until you've become completely associated with it. Keep in mind, though, that the topic you choose must be the one that matters to you the most and that you can support wholeheartedly through a sustained effort. After all, you'll be living with this issue for a long time to come.

October 25

❖ *Celebrate something.*

Today's an important holiday that people in your program or at your institution need to celebrate. You didn't know that? Well, that's because you're going to *make* today a holiday. Identify a cause for celebration so that others can develop their own enthusiasm for it. For example, you could celebrate this year's enrollment figures. Regard it as an achievement to be recognized no matter whether they're going up, have stopped going down, are declining at a lower rate than in previous years, or have helped you improve your student-to-faculty ratio. Celebrate a grant regardless of whether it was recently awarded, the proposal has just been completed, or it has been identified as an area for which the proposal is about to be drafted. Honor recent faculty publications, conference presentations, innovative contributions to instruction, exceptional examples of service, or whatever else has made a difference in your area. The point is that there's always something to celebrate, and most of us don't stop frequently enough to recognize the important achievements that are going on all around us. If you start doing so, you'll find that you can have impromptu holidays on nearly any day of the year.

October 26

❖ *Open yourself to persuasion.*

Good academic leaders don't just ask the right kind of questions. They also listen thoughtfully to the answers, and if what they learn causes them to see matters from a better perspective, they allow themselves to be persuaded. We've all known leaders who seemed excessively easy to persuade; at times it appeared as though they tended to agree with whomever they talked to last. But we've also probably also known leaders who confused persistence with obstinacy and refused to see the merit in anyone's ideas other than their own. Today's suggestion is to make a conscious effort to be open to persuasion whenever it is warranted. Even in areas in which you have the utmost confidence in your judgment, listen carefully to what others tell you and assess their views objectively. Give yourself permission to feel that perhaps differing views may be right and that you won't be dismissed as weak or vacillating if you abandon an ill-conceived position. To put it another way, make today's activity an exercise in active listening. Even more important, make it an exercise in active understanding.

October 27

❖ Ask, "Why?"

Every now and then it can be beneficial to pause and think, "Now why exactly am I doing this?" You'll find this question posed in several ways throughout this guide. For instance, you'll be encouraged to remind yourself why you wanted your current position. You'll consider your long-range and short-term goals. And you'll reflect on the various ways in which your institution and community are benefited by what you do. Today, try to approach the "why?" question from the broadest possible perspective: Why does higher education even exist? What's the goal of the modern college or university? How do you define its fundamental mission? Some people might say that the mission of all higher education is ultimately economic: colleges and universities help their graduates get better jobs and thus contribute significantly to the regional economy. Other people might say that the mission of higher education is ultimately cultural: colleges and universities pass on and critique the values of their societies. Still others might say that the mission of higher education is ultimately intellectual: colleges and universities train students to think critically and creatively regardless of the area in which its graduates will apply those skills. Of course, you can always take the easy way out and say that higher education does all of these things and much more—that it's a false dilemma to imply that colleges and universities primarily do one thing and not the other. But each of us, when we're being absolutely candid, is convinced that some role for higher education is the highest or the best. How does your belief of "why you're here" affect the decisions that you'll make today?

October 28

❖ *Make time fly.*

As children, we all learn that time seems to drag when we're bored but speeds up considerably when we're enjoying ourselves. This common childhood wisdom can be your salvation when you find yourself stuck in an unproductive meeting. The next time you're involved in a process that seems to be taking far longer than it should or involves material that may be important but can be described only as tedious, see if you can think of ways of making the time pass more pleasantly for yourself and others. Suggest that the committee break into subgroups, with each subgroup charged with developing a proposal to address one specific part of the problem. Offer to reward the committee member who comes up with the best suggestion or gives the shortest report at the next meeting. Promise to bring treats to the next session if you can get through today's agenda in record time. What you propose will depend on the nature of the committee's task and the personalities of its members, but you can almost always think of some creative way to make required meetings livelier and more enjoyable. This task becomes more difficult when you're not in charge of the group yourself. Even then, however, if no other solution comes to mind, give yourself permission to reclaim an occasional free moment for yourself. Mentally outline a report you need to write, establish your priorities for tomorrow, or consider the points that you'll address during your next appointment. As long as it doesn't interfere with your own contributions to the committee, spending your time on a project that you regard as more important to you will help make the time pass more quickly.

October 29

❖ *Become your own life coach.*

People turn to different kinds of coaches when they want to improve their performance in some way. Athletic coaches, drama coaches, and singing coaches are familiar to almost everyone. Less common, at least in higher education, are executive coaches (who help those who work in the corporate world achieve both personal and institutional goals) and conflict coaches (who help mediate differences in a constructive manner). Perhaps the greatest responsibility falls to the life coach: the consultant who is hired to help people balance their personal and professional lives, establish clear goals for the future, and cope with stress. Unlike other types of therapists who focus on overcoming issues from the past, life coaches deal almost exclusively with present choices and perspectives, as well as the expectation that the future will be as satisfying as possible. Working one-on-one with a life coach can be a time-consuming and expensive proposition, but in your role as an academic leader, you have most of the skills you need to serve as your own life coach. Consider your life and career, and imagine that it belonged to someone else. What would you advise in order for that person to achieve greater success and happiness? When you review your actions as though you were an objective witness, which aspects of your life seem out of balance or contrary to the values you claim are important? When you consider your own justifications for your mistakes and failures, which of them seem to be mere excuses? How might you urge someone just like you to rearrange priorities so as to achieve more of what will ultimately be most important?

October 30

❖ *Decide how you make decisions.*

There's no universally correct way to make a decision. Some administrators "go with their gut," while others prefer to review every possible alternative. Some people like to talk matters through with a group of close advisors, while others need to ponder issues alone. Consider your own decision-making style, and try to identify any patterns you fall into whenever a difficult choice is looming. Do you find advice from others helpful, or does it simply annoy you when others give you their opinions while you're trying to make a decision? Do you find that you use entirely different processes in different situations, depending, for instance, on whether the issue in question is personal or professional, major or mundane? The purpose of today's exercise is not to change the way you make decisions, but to become more intentional about your decision-making process. This insight could prove to be invaluable the next time you find yourself perplexed and don't know how to begin to decide among various alternatives.

October 31

❖ *Be frightened.*

Halloween is the day when people traditionally dress in costumes, tell frightening stories, and delight in the pleasure of being (safely) scared. In keeping with today's spirit (or perhaps *spirits*), spend some time thinking about the things that frighten you professionally. What could possibly occur that, if you had it in your power to prevent, you'd never want your program or institution to suffer? What potential disasters do you fear for your personal or professional life? Your goal in thinking through these scenarios isn't to scare yourself, but rather to make sure you're taking the appropriate steps to ensure that these unnerving possibilities remain unlikely to occur. For instance, if you regard the death of a student as the single worst thing that could happen in your academic area, how frequently do you review safety procedures with your students and verify that your facilities are as safe as possible? If you would regard the public humiliation that would result from a financial scandal as the worst possible thing that could happen to you professionally, how careful are you to keep all of your financial records up to date and to reimburse your institution for even small expenses that benefited you more personally than professionally? Each administrator is likely to have his or her own individual story about the worst possible thing that could occur to his or her school, program, or life. Your goal today should be to assess what you're doing in order to prevent your own personal horror show from becoming all too real.

November

November 1

❖ *Do something that really matters.*

As we've already seen, it's easy to devote day after day solely to meeting deadlines and crossing items off our to-do lists. That type of approach results in getting a lot of things done, but it can often leave you feeling that you haven't really a made a positive difference through your efforts. As a result, today's suggestion is to select one project or goal that matters to you, and then make it your priority until that dream becomes a reality. Naturally, it may not be possible to complete this entire task today. Big, important achievements usually take time. But what it is possible to do is to make a firm commitment that you're going to achieve this goal and that today's the day when you'll get the project well under way. Prepare a clear and realistic timetable for completing the task, allowing plenty of extra time for unforeseen contingencies. By making a commitment to do something that really matters, you'll reduce the likelihood that you'll reach the end of the academic year asking, "Where in the world did all of the time go?"

November 2

❖ *Spend time with your best faculty members.*

One of the frustrations of many academic administrators is that they end up spending most of their time on the weakest members of their faculty or staff. These are

69

frequently the people who always wish to raise a complaint or whom their supervisor has to see because a complaint's been raised about them. They can tie up an entire day by requiring others to mediate their conflicts. When they have annual reviews that go awry, they take up even more time justifying and rationalizing their poor performance, and then they can require additional effort as the supervisor or a designee coaches and trains them to be more successful next year. These are the squeaky wheels who expect to be greased if only they keep on squeaking a little longer and a little louder. The problem with this common occurrence is that it can divert us from spending more time with the people who deserve it the most: our best performers. It's our outstanding teachers, stellar researchers, and excellent community citizens who can help us achieve our most important goals. In return, these are the people who can also benefit from having us prepare them for even greater leadership roles. So, make an effort today to direct a significant amount of time to the stars on your faculty rather than to the people who have the most complaints or cause you the most problems. Resolve that at least for today, you'll spend time building on success rather than putting out fires.

November 3

❖ *Use only positive words.*

It's amazing how negative most people are about most things most of the time. As an experiment, listen to a conversation, and count the number of sentences that are spoken before someone utters a complaint, criticism, disparaging remark, veiled insult, or even a not-so-veiled insult. Negativity feeds on negativity, and after living and working in such an environment, we might find ourselves becoming more cynical and pessimistic. For this reason, today's goal is to spend the entire day making nothing but positive remarks. Rather than criticism, offer constructive advice; rather than focusing on what you can't do, highlight what's possible. You probably won't find people responding to this change instantly by becoming more positive in their own language, but they may begin fewer sentences with, "The problem with that is . . ." Long-established habits take a long time to break. But the attitude that you bring to your work in this exercise may well make you feel more energetic and positive about the challenges you are facing. And if you feel more energetic and positive, the work that you do will end up being better, more innovative, and more enjoyable, too.

November 4

❖ *Discourage end runs.*

Decisions in any organization should always be made at the lowest possible level. The reason for following this policy isn't to create unnecessary barriers between employees and administrators, but to make sure that decisions are made by people who are best informed about specific details and most likely to be affected by the choices that are made. Administrators who agree to intervene in a matter that should have been resolved at a lower level are implicitly giving permission for all matters of this sort to be brought to their attention; they'll soon find themselves inundated with minor or routine issues as a result. By allowing lower levels of the organization to make decisions, you're empowering others in a way that builds their own leadership skills. You're acting as a role model to discourage micromanagement, and you're eliminating the impression that certain people have special access to you. Of course, mistakes will be made when others are empowered to make decisions, but making mistakes is one very important way in which future leaders learn the art of good academic administration.

November 5

❖ *Know your legislators.*

No matter whether your institution is public or private, actions taken by federal and state legislators affect your work and the experience your students will have. Today, make sure you can name all the senators and representatives who serve your area at the federal level, as well as all the people who represent your region at the state level. Do you know how to contact them when you need to? Do you know all the positions they have taken with regard to higher education? Would you recognize any of these legislators if you passed them on the street? Knowing your legislators can be critical to promoting the long-term interests of your program or institution. So before the end or the day, be sure you can name all of the people who represent you *and* articulate their views on education in general, funding for higher education, and their probable level of awareness of the programs that you supervise.

November 6

❖ *Improve your telephone log.*

A telephone log is a simple record of the people you've spoken to on the phone that indicates whether you placed or received the call, at what time the call occurred, and the range of subjects discussed. You can keep a basic log on a legal pad, but with all of the advantages of electronic searching, maintaining telephone logs as a database, a spreadsheet, or part of a calendar program may be preferable. In fact, certain software applications come with built-in templates for a telephone log, making it extremely easy to establish one if you've never done so. The advantage of a telephone log is that it takes away the guesswork involved with remembering when a certain call occurred, what was discussed, and which action items arose from that discussion. In certain rare cases (for example, when someone claims that you never made an important request or that the two of you had never reached an agreement), the log can be invaluable in proving that a conversation took place. Today's task therefore is simple: start a telephone log if you don't have one, and if you already maintain a log, find some way of improving it. Your improvement might consist of converting a paper log to an electronic format, expanding the information that your log contains (the duration of each call, color-coding entries to distinguish personal from business calls, linking log entries to contact information in your address book), or streamlining a format that has become burdensome. A well-maintained telephone log can improve your efficiency by allowing you to recognize how much time you're spending on personal calls and at what time of day and when in the academic year your call volume tends to be the highest.

November 7

❖ *Envision a better future.*

Complete the following sentence: "A year from today, the one thing that I hope will be different is . . ." What's the first thing you think of? The answer you provide is your key not only to envisioning a better future but to go about creating it. Sometimes when we picture what we'd like to occur, we imagine eliminating an obstacle that's holding us back from an easier or more fulfilling existence. But sometimes we imagine an exciting new possibility that would allow us to achieve more of our potential and become more engaged in our work or our personal lives. If the thing you most wish would change is some aspect of your personal life, regard this goal as particularly significant because those areas of dissatisfaction or aspiration tend to affect our entire outlook, and have an impact on everything we do at work, at home, and in our relationships. But also give attention to something specific that you'd like to change in your professional environment. If the change you have in mind involves someone else, think about how you might alter or improve your relationship with the person as an initial step toward making things better. Then complete today's activity by coming up with at least three concrete actions you can take immediately to begin bringing about whatever change you would most like to see.

November 8

❖ *Think holistically.*

Because this book deals with the small changes we can make in order to become more effective administrators, it may seem as though this guide is encouraging you to become preoccupied with minutiae. While a central theme of *Academic Leadership Day by Day* is that a series of fairly small improvements can add up to some significant results, it's important for every academic leader to balance concern for details with an ability to see overall patterns. As a step toward achieving this goal, spend some time today thinking about the single biggest challenge that you believe higher education faces. Don't remain satisfied with the first answer you come up with. Keep challenging yourself by thinking of different possibilities. Consider how you'd respond to someone who disputed your view that what you have in mind is the single greatest problem facing higher education. What makes the issue you've identified so significant? Who is most harmed because of this issue, and why is this problem so difficult to solve? If the challenge you've identified can't be overcome completely, how do other colleges and universities manage or isolate its severity? If you could implement a sweeping change affecting all of higher education, how would you seek to respond to the problem you've identified today?

November 9

❖ *Learn something new about academic freedom.*

There is probably no other issue as central to the identity of Western universities as academic freedom. And yet the case law devoted to issues of academic freedom continues to expand, and many people have only the haziest understanding of what this concept actually entails. Ask a faculty member to define academic freedom, and then pose the same question to a member of your institution's governing board, and you're likely to receive extremely different answers. Devote at least a portion of today to investigating some aspect of academic freedom that you don't feel you've completely mastered. You might explore its historical development in the academy, recent cases where institutions have been accused of impinging on a faculty member's academic freedom, or the differences between professorial and institutional academic freedom. In what types of cases are the courts most willing to intervene, and what situations do they prefer to leave to the college or university itself? Have advances in either instructional or research technology complicated issues of academic freedom recently? Have certain cases recently received a great deal of media attention and thus renewed the public debate about academic freedom? Remember that you don't have to master this entire topic today, merely increase your understanding of one particular area.

November 10

❖ *Raise the bar.*

Throughout this (and every other) year, you'll have many opportunities to observe the way in which people live up (or down) to the standards we expect of them. The faculty member who's identified as a Wunderkind early in his or her career frequently excels because that's exactly what's expected, while the colleague who's identified as a problem often feels obliged to engage in behavior that's problematic. With this principle as your basis, think of some area of your responsibilities in which it seems possible to raise standards and thus achieve better results. Naturally certain areas you might think of will either be outside your sphere of responsibility or require a committee decision before they can be implemented. But every administrator also has certain decisions that can be made at his or her own discretion. Identify one of these areas today, and consider how increasing expectations could be beneficial to your program or institution. Rather than merely imposing these new standards unilaterally, discuss them in advance with the stakeholders who will be affected. Justify your reasons for feeling that it's time to raise the bar in this area, and try to build a broad base of support for increased standards. Naturally, you'll want to give people sufficient time to meet your higher expectations, but keep your focus on the important benefits that will result from this improvement.

November 11

❖ *Expand access.*

One of the great achievements of higher education in recent years is the expanded access it provides for people to receive information, training, and increased opportunities. Whereas once only a small percentage of students were educated beyond high school, today access to a college or university education is no longer solely for the elite. This improved access to educational opportunities plays a significant role in economic, cultural, and intellectual development, helping to transform society at the same time that it transforms the lives of individuals. With this concept in mind, think of at least one important way in which you could improve the access that others have to your institution, program, or you. (In certain cases, it can be almost as crucial for students and faculty members to have timely and direct access to the appropriate administrator as it can be for them to have direct access to other resources of the school.) Your idea doesn't have to be as grandiose as a major new scholarship program for disadvantaged students, although that's a fine idea; it simply has to be a practical way for the people who depend on the information and services of the area you supervise to obtain easier access to what they need. New technologies are developed all the time that make services, which would have been prohibitively expensive only a few years earlier, easy to obtain at little or no cost. Approach each situation today by asking what you could be doing in order to provide more people with greater access to the benefits that your program or institution offers.

November 12

❧ *Stop and smell the roses.*

The injunction *carpe diem* is usually translated as "seize the day." In Latin, however, the verb *carpo* actually means something closer to "I pick" or "I pluck" than "I seize." In other words, it's a verb of harvesting or cultivation rather than of forceful grasping, even though the ancient Romans—who possessed both a huge army and empire—had plenty of words to describe seizing things too. The poet Horace, who first used the expression *carpe diem* in one of his odes (1.11), was speaking about the desirability of living each day to the fullest, not necessarily about striking while the iron is hot. The focus of the words in this expression should thus be to gather the beauty of each day into a bouquet of life experiences; if you spend all your time planning for tomorrow, you never get to enjoy today. With this somewhat different sense of a familiar expression in mind, devote a few moments today to enjoying the flowers all around you. Who are the colleagues and coworkers who make your life easier and whom you don't thank often enough? What personal goals have you been able to achieve in your job that you might once have regarded as wonderful but impossible dreams? What brings you joy or satisfaction in your career? Don't let the day go by without considering how fortunate you are to be doing just what you are today. Even your challenges and frustrations are a gift because they give you the chance to improve higher education in at least some way.

November 13

❖ *Think like a novice.*

Whenever you first become interested in a skill or subject, the possibilities seem endless. You don't yet know what you can't do because you haven't yet learned what's impossible. You don't even know what the "right" way of doing something should be. It's only as you become more knowledgeable in that skill or subject that you begin to narrow your focus to a few "acceptable" answers or "appropriate" ways of doing things. And yet incredible changes are possible if you approach each task as a beginner, unrestricted by the limitations of prior knowledge. After all, the great jazz guitarist Django Reinhardt (1910–1953) developed his own unique style because no one ever taught him that it was "impossible" to play as he did. The architect Michael Ventris (1922–1956) deciphered the Linear B tablets in part because he brought an outsider's view to the subject and hadn't accepted the common assumption that their language "couldn't" be Greek. In the study of Zen, the concept of *shoshin*, or "beginner's mind," refers to the practice of approaching each experience without preconceived expectations or limitations on what might be possible. Today try to address each situation you encounter as a novice would, not rejecting any idea as impractical but considering it and wondering, "Why not?"

November 14

❖ *Seek common ground.*

If there are ongoing conflicts or disputes in the programs that you supervise, today is the day to begin healing them. Work with the different factions, at first independently and then together as a group, not to resolve all the issues immediately but to find at least some small area of common ground. No matter how diametrically opposed the various perspectives may be, there must be some point on which they can agree. Get the various sides talking about the priority you all place on helping students, achieving significant results in your research, making an important difference in the world, or any other topic that all sides necessarily view in a similar manner. Then see if you can build outward from that point of agreement by saying something like, "Even though each of us has a different idea about how the new program should be developed, it's clear that every single one of us is committed to the success of the new curriculum and the role it can play in the lives of our students." Once people are brought back to the point where they share basic values with others, it becomes far more difficult for them to sustain their animosity over implementation issues. The differences of opinion are then revealed to be matters of individual preferences, not fundamental assumptions, and most people understand (even if they don't always admit) that preferences often have to be negotiated in a department, college, or university. Continue these discussions until you can reasonably say to all participants, "You know, it's clear to me now that we're not really discussing opposing ideas; we're merely examining various details about how to achieve a shared goal. At root I'm sensing a lot of agreement about the objective we're trying to achieve."

November 15

❖ *Don't take it personally.*

Receiving criticism is part and parcel of being an administrator. Some of the criticism you receive from others is important and should be taken seriously; it can prevent you from making mistakes or failing to explore all sides of an issue. Some of the criticism will simply be the result of workplace dynamics; grumbling about the boss fulfills a common need, and as long as these complaints remain harmless venting, they're not something you should go out of your way to discourage. Also, some of the criticism you receive will come from chronic complainers—the people who always seem to have an issue to whine about. As soon as you respond to them and fix one problem, they'll be back in your office finding fault with something else. There's a common theme running through all these different types of criticism: as we saw back on September 17, none of this is really about you, although it can feel like that at the time. The complaints may be about your policies or actions, the sheer fact that you're the person's supervisor, or the need that a chronic complainer has to vent about something, but none of it is really about you as a person. Another way of looking at this is to realize that there's you, and then there's the administrative position that you hold at your school. It can be easy at times to confuse those two, but they really are different. If you reflect on each complaint objectively and ask, "What's this criticism

really about?" you'll find that almost always, something
else prompted the person's statement. As an administrator,
you're often just an easy target. So don't take it personally.
It's part of your job, and it now gives you an opportunity to
ask, "What can I do to help make this situation better?"

November 16

> ❖ *Establish boundaries.*

As an academic leader, it often feels as though you're
on the job seven days a week, twenty-four hours a day. And
in many ways you are. But administrators who don't establish a sense of boundary between their own lives and the
contributions they make to their institutions run the risk
of low job satisfaction and a high rate of burnout. Review
your responsibilities today, and give yourself permission to
establish clear boundaries between work and your personal life. Remember that not every lunch has to be a
working lunch; take some time to go off by yourself or to
chat with people you really want to be with, not just those
you have to be with. Resolve not to take work home with
you tonight. Or if that's impossible because of the nature
of your responsibilities, resolve not to take certain *kinds* of
work home with you. In the future, it may be possible for
you to establish a plan where you'll take some work home
only on certain days of the week. Starting today, delegate
more freely, particularly when there are others who are

better trained or more capable of handling certain kinds of issues than you are. Understand that refusing to be drawn too deeply into other people's personal concerns doesn't mean that you're not a caring person; it just means you recognize that others will sometimes be better served if you can remain detached from problems they really have to solve by themselves. Keep in mind that you can't give others what you don't have yourself. So if failure to establish boundaries means that you are depriving yourself of energy and a sense of calm, you're not going to be in a position to help other people even if you try.

November 17

❖ *Accommodate differences.*

Everyone has a way in which he or she learns best. Some people tend to be visual learners and benefit from seeing diagrams or illustrations, then recalling what a page or computer screen looks like when they're trying to remember information. Others learn better in an auditory form, listening to lectures in class, on CDs, or with mp3 players and "hearing" the information in their heads whenever they review it. Still others learn better by experience and thrive when they are exposed to simulations, experiments, and other hands-on activities. We could break down these learning styles even further, distinguishing people who learn best when working independently from those who study better in groups, those who require absolute quiet when they study versus those who prefer music or background noise, those who like to invent new things as opposed to those who prefer to apply proven principles, and so on. But the central point is clear: learning styles vary a great deal, and the best sort of learning environment is the one that can accommodate as many of these different approaches as possible. For this reason, review the programs that you supervise today, and try to determine how well each of them serves the needs of visual, auditory, experiential, independent, social, discovery-oriented, and implementation-oriented learners. If you could introduce even one slight improvement to the learning environment in your area, what would it be?

November 18

❖ *Identify your biggest challenge.*

No academic leader is without flaws. We all have our areas of weakness and rise to our current positions by compensating for those limitations in some way. For instance, a good dean knows how to select associate deans and program directors based on a need to complement, not unnecessarily duplicate, his or her own abilities. Moreover, if you've ever interviewed for another administrative appointment, you're almost certain to be asked, "What's your greatest weakness?" The standard way of replying

to this question—take a strength and describe it as
though it were a weakness ("Sometimes I'm just too
dedicated to my job")—is a fairly transparent ruse. A far
better response is to acknowledge a genuine limitation,
but then state how you've been able to overcome this
difficulty. In order to do that, however, you first have
to know precisely what your weaknesses are. So spend
a little time today candidly assessing the areas that
provide you with challenge and developing practical
approaches to address those imperfections as creatively as
possible.

November 19

·::· *Make the first move.*

We sometimes reach an impasse in situations because
neither party in the discussion is willing to make any
concession. In the worst of these stalemates, that lack of
progress can continue for months, perhaps even years.
Even in less extreme situations, we may find ourselves
giving up on an endeavor that would actually be of great
benefit to our students or faculty members because we've
reached a point where progress seems to be impossible.
If you can identify a situation like this in your own area,
today's your opportunity to make the first move. Revisit
the issue and weigh the competing priorities. See if you can
identify a concession you can make to others that is less

important to you than the overall good that will result from moving this project forward. If enough time has passed since your last discussions about this subject, you may even find that positions about which other parties were so adamant before now have become much more flexible. After all, they too may have realized that a greater good is being hindered by a relatively minor inconvenience. Yet even if your overture is rejected, you'll still have the satisfaction of knowing that you made an appropriate effort on behalf of an important goal. Make a note to revisit the issue again several weeks or months from now and to follow your first move, where necessary, with second or third moves in order to achieve an important benefit for your program or institution.

November 20

> ❖ *Reflect on the relationship between students and faculty members.*

The relationship that students have with faculty members is wonderful and utterly unique. A little like the relationship between a parent and child, the professor-student relationship also bears some similarities to the bond formed between a senior and junior colleague, a supervisor and an employee, a mentor and a protégé, and a physician and a patient. When all goes well, the student thrives and graduates from the school with warm and cherished memories; when all goes wrong, rancor—and occasionally even lawsuits—result. So spend some time today recalling the best and the worst faculty-student relationships you have known throughout your career. What were the features that seemed to characterize the relationships that turned out particularly well? Are there similar themes and patterns that illustrate what caused certain relationships to sour? For instance, is there a clear line that distinguishes warm and supportive caring from inappropriate familiarity and lack of boundaries? Can you easily distinguish between setting extremely high standards for students and being so excessively demanding that they become frustrated and demoralized? Consider what you've learned from studying these patterns of good and bad student-faculty relations, and reflect on what you might do in your area in order to foster more of the productive relationships while minimizing the problematic ones.

November 21

❖ *Examine workload carefully.*

Because of the type of work performed at colleges and universities, it can be easy for people from outside the academy to misunderstand the nature of academic workload. When it is said that a faculty member is teaching "only" two or three classes a year, people sometimes say, "No wonder college is so expensive! You're paying someone a full-time salary for only a few hours of work a week." When such remarks are made, we tend to lapse into our oft-repeated remarks about faculty workload being far more than time spent in a classroom. Even teaching, we say, requires a great deal of preparation before and grading after class, and that still doesn't take into account the other contributions expected from faculty. But even as we strive hard to explain the complexities of academic workload to our external constituents, we also need to be sure that we ourselves don't misunderstand the many dimensions of faculty responsibilities today. Over the years, faculty work has grown far beyond such traditional duties as teaching courses, performing research, and serving on committees; it now encompasses recruiting potential students and meeting with donors, keeping abreast of new technologies for instruction and scholarship, converting materials to an expanding array of learning platforms, engaging in strategic planning, speaking to alumni, and a host of other duties. Although most faculty contracts are for nine or tenth months of the year, no one expects faculty members to stop working and developing their skills when they're not under contract. For all of these reasons, devote time today to reviewing the genuine complexity of faculty workload in your area.

November 22

⁂ *Discover new sources of administrative insight.*

Almost endless resources are available about ways to improve academic administration. New books, periodicals, electronic resources, workshops or conferences, and other opportunities are continually becoming available. Investigate these resources today, and make it a point of identifying a few good leads that you didn't know about yesterday. Do an Internet search on such words as "academic administrators conference" or "department chair publication," and see what pops up. You may discover that there's information available on a topic that has long interested or puzzled you. You may also discover new outlets where you can share with others your own best practices or insights into administrative policies. No one ever has enough time to read everything available on professional development. But it's important to take time every now and then to discover a few new resources that are particularly relevant to what we do as a way of helping us to do our jobs better.

November 23

⁂ *Glow with pride.*

Review your faculty's recent accomplishments today. Look at the number of grants they received this year, the number of books they published, how many articles were published in top-tier journals, and how many national or international conferences accepted their proposals. Examine student ratings of instruction, peer reviews, unsolicited letters of commendation, and the teaching awards your faculty members received as a way of reminding yourself how excellent they are in the classroom, studio, and lab. Think back to any occasion where someone praised an instructor in your area for a truly innovative or selfless act, and try to picture some of the times when one of your faculty members made a important difference at your institution. But don't merely review and remember these accomplishments; your goal today should be to *revel* in them. Remember that your faculty is an important part—probably the single most important part—of what makes your college or university a success. Allow yourself to feel a genuine sense of pride in having the opportunity to work with such a talented group of people. Then let that pride radiate today in everything you do.

November 24

❖ *Embrace your greatest frustration.*

Each of us is aware of something that causes us frustration in our professional lives. It may be a skill like public speaking or visionary thinking that we find particularly challenging. It may be an issue that we regard as extremely important but that others don't approach as enthusiastically as we might like. It may even be a person with whom we have a personality conflict or such a strong difference of opinion that even simple conversation becomes exasperating. Whomever or whatever you identify as your greatest frustration, try today to find some way in which your life actually benefits from this often-maddening relationship. In other words, the skill that we can't master no matter how hard we try may be precisely what keeps us from becoming too confident in our own abilities. The issue that others don't care about as passionately as we do may cause us to reexamine our own understanding of this subject or discover new ways of explaining its significance to our stakeholders. The person whom we regard as our greatest irritant may actually be the very person who causes us to work harder, think more creatively, or apply our talents to new areas. By embracing our frustrations, we can help transform our workplace from a constant source of provocation to a beneficial environment where we're continually tested and improved. Since we can't usually change the person or situation, the easiest thing to change is our attitude. And our attitude may well have been the problem all along.

November 25

❖ *Build a team.*

Any organization (or even any subunit within it) is much more than the sum of its parts. A team benefits from both the individual talents of all its members and the synergy that results from the unique blend of their abilities. Sometimes colleges and departments seem to develop their own chemistry, helping them generate high morale and an extremely productive environment. At other times, units may need a little encouragement before they develop a supportive working relationship. Review today your own impressions of the area you supervise, and try to identify at least three or four concrete steps you can take in order to promote team building. For instance, have you encouraged people to recognize and celebrate each other's accomplishments? Have you given those who work for you a sense that they're all part of something truly significant? Does every member of your area feel that an achievement by the whole group is also a personal accomplishment, and vice versa? Do you discuss shared goals on a regular basis? Do you celebrate when progress is made toward achieving these goals? Do you make a conscious effort to improve morale and encourage a team spirit, or do you expect it to arise as an accidental by-product from day-to-day activities? Do you ever hold social events where members of your area can bond with one another in ways not directly related to their work? Have you as a leader demonstrated to your employees that you're personally committed to their success? As you reflect on these questions, think of strategies you can implement that suit your own personality and the nature of the people you work with. Aim for an approach the best suits the personality of your team.

November 26

❖ *Share your story.*

Your individual story includes many different plot-lines. It contains the plot of your background or childhood and the path that ultimately brought you to an administrative career. It consists, too, of the history of your program or institution and the heritage on which you build every day. If someone were to ask you to tell your story in five minutes or less, what would you say? What are the most important things for someone to know about you, the academic area you serve, your administrative philosophy, and the motivations that inspire you from day to day? Take some time today to clarify your story in your own mind, and then choose someone with whom to share it. Notice which aspects of your story seem most important to the other person, which details appeared to come as a surprise, and which elements (if any) seem superficial when you say them aloud. Remember, too, that your story is an evolving narrative, and you'll want to revisit it from time to time in order to determine how your personal plotline may be changing for you and where you are experiencing the most growth. Finally, always keep in mind that sharing your story should not be an exercise in egoism. It is, rather, a practice that helps you develop greater self-understanding, a prerequisite to effective leadership. After all, it's nearly impossible to help others become the best people they can be if you yourself don't know who you are.

November 27

❖ *Clarify responsibilities.*

One of the things that people most complain about in any professional setting is not knowing exactly what's expected of them. They may feel uncertain as to precisely what their responsibilities are, which decisions they're authorized to make on their own, and in what areas they may exercise initiative without infringing on someone else's duties. It can be maddening to realize that you were expected to do something you never realized was a part of your responsibilities, and it can be almost as frustrating to learn that you *could* have made a decision that no one ever told you that you were empowered to make. For this reason, survey the people who work in your area, and have a brief conversation with each of them about their specific job responsibilities. Make it clear that they haven't done anything wrong; it's just that you want to "make sure we're all on the same page" about who's doing what and where each person's area of responsibility begins and ends. You may find that certain people assume they're in charge of certain matters that really need to be addressed at different levels of the institution, while others feel that particular duties are not their job even though, as their supervisor, you really believe they should be performing these tasks. Clearing the air in this way can sometimes cause some hurt feelings or grumbling for a while. But if you handle the situation with tact and diplomacy, you'll end up with a staff that better understands what you need each person to do, and why.

November 28

❖ *Change your environment.*

Working in the same surroundings day after day can put you in a rut, making it difficult to identify new possibilities or embrace innovative ideas. Several times throughout this year, we'll look at ways of preventing the familiar from becoming too routine, from reorganizing your personal workspace to consulting with students about how your office or classroom environment might be improved. Today we'll explore a different strategy for achieving a similar goal: get away from your work environment entirely, at least for a time. One of the reasons that off-campus retreats encourage people to think in new ways is that people are suddenly immersed in a new (and usually very attractive) environment. So think of today as your personal mini-retreat. You can perform this exercise alone, with a few close associates, or with your entire staff if you prefer. The most important thing is to find a physical space that's significantly different from your usual workspace and that permits you to view matters in a new way. For example, if you usually work in an area that's chaotic and cluttered, seek a sparse and clean space. If your work environment is filled with bright, artificial light, try to find somewhere that's calm, serene, and less harsh to the eyes. If it's not possible to organize this event today due to your own plans or the schedules of others, then at least use today to choose a time and location for a mini-retreat in the near future. Experiment with a few possibilities in order to discover how changing your environment can help you change people's minds, including your own.

November 29

❖ *Take a chance on someone.*

Effective administration balances making responsible decisions with taking calculated risks. Today's activity is devoted to the risk side of this equation. The goal is to take a chance on someone who either has not yet had a chance to prove his or her value to your area or, having had the chance, was unsuccessful at it. The central idea behind today's suggestion is that if we entrust responsibilities only to those who have already demonstrated their effectiveness, we eventually come to rely on an increasingly tighter circle of people who are expected to handle every important assignment. But developing leadership means providing opportunities to people who have not yet had them, as well as placing confidence again in those who have let us down in the past. After all, people do learn from their earlier mistakes, and even when that type of growth doesn't seem possible, they may develop improved judgment and efficiency as they mature. It's quite possible that you wouldn't be where you are today if someone hadn't taken a chance on you, so return the favor and commit yourself to taking a chance on someone else.

November 30

❖ *Provide context.*

Members of any organization can begin to feel as though they're sometimes expected to carry out instructions that are developed randomly or completely unrelated to one another. It's easier to understand the big picture when you're seeing an institution from higher levels in its hierarchy, and employees whose day-to-day duties lie in the trenches may have little or no idea why a new procedure was established. Today, take a step toward better communication by clearly explaining the significance of some goal or project that's important to you. Articulate as explicitly as you can the benefits that will result and how those benefits relate to the overall mission of your program or the entire institution. Then be open to questions that others may ask. They may see aspects of the issue that are invisible to you because the nature of your work is different from theirs. Even if the answers to their questions seem overly obvious or trivial, take these questions seriously. You may have been living with this project or goal in mind for quite a long time now, while to others it may be a new and unfamiliar idea. Let people see why it's important to accomplish the objective you've outlined or to change their procedures in the manner you've proposed. Even if they don't come away agreeing with the change completely, they're likely to perform the work more effectively since they now have a better understanding of the context in which the new policy has been adopted.

December

December 1

⁘ Prepare for the home stretch.

Entering the last month of the calendar year serves as a good reminder of other deadlines that are probably looming. Most institutions that follow the North American system are nearing the end of the fall term. There may well be projects and commitments you've undertaken that you'll need to complete soon. And even the close of the entire academic year will be here before you know it. Today's suggestion is thus to reflect on how you deal with situations where important deadlines are near and the pressure is building. Do you find yourself benefiting from an extra burst of creativity due to the excitement of crunch time? Or does the stress of deadlines cause you so much anxiety that you're unable to be as effective as you'd like to be? Do you regularly meet target dates (perhaps hitting Send or overnighting the documents at the last possible moment), or are you likely to ask for an extension every now and then? Or are you the sort of person who completes projects days, perhaps even weeks, ahead of time (and then becomes annoyed when the person who receives your report misplaces it because it arrived so much earlier than it was expected)? The point of today's activity isn't to encourage you to plan better or start earlier if you tend to miss deadlines—even though that may be very good advice—but rather to cause you to study your own responses to periods of high pressure and understand your

103

work habits better. By gaining greater insight into how you are likely to react when a due date is pending, you'll be in the best position to take full advantage of how this habit works well for you and how to compensate when your usual practice is likely to cause problems.

December 2

❖ *Identify an opportunity*.

In a traditional SWOT analysis, organizations identify the strengths, weaknesses, opportunities, and threats that face them. Strengths and weaknesses are internal factors that are specific to that particular organization and its resources. Opportunities and threats are external matters, resulting from the environment in which the organization operates and the other institutions with which it competes. Although this type of analysis is useful, completing it properly involves so much brainstorming and research that it's impossible to complete in the few minutes you have set aside for these daily suggestions. So instead, spend a few moments today identifying *one specific opportunity* that exists for your program or institution. For instance, the demographics in your region may suggest that a large influx of traditionally aged students will be seeking degrees within the next few years, and you could capitalize on this future opportunity by beginning to prepare for it now. Or new corporations may be expanding their base of operations in your area, providing an opportunity for new internships and cooperative programs. Your alumni may soon be entering their peak earning years, suggesting that fundraising efforts should start to be redirected toward the graduates of your program. The number of retired people in your region may be increasing, providing an opportunity for your program to engage them through educational and cultural activities and thus perhaps introducing your discipline to a new source of external funding. No matter what your environment is, there is almost certainly some distinctive trend that you can begin taking better advantage of today.

December 3

❖ *Remember that having fun matters.*

No one will deny that higher education administration is important and serious work. Colleges and universities radically change people's lives for the better, offering new opportunities for students, expanding the worldview of everyone associated with them, producing research that has long-lasting benefit, serving as a nexus for cultural activities, and providing a positive model of a community where merit, talent, and achievement matter far more than do race, creed, or socioeconomic background. Nevertheless, although the work that academic leaders do is serious, it's not essential that those of us who work in higher education be serious every very single moment of every single day. In fact, academic leaders can undermine their own authority by taking themselves too seriously and not enjoying the lighthearted pleasure that can be derived from a well-rounded college experience. For this reason, make it a priority today to have a good time, no matter what tasks are facing you. Even more important, give those who work with you license to have fun on the job as well. As long as goals are met and the work is done, there's absolutely no harm—and even a great deal of benefit—in creating a work environment where people enjoy coming to the office every day. Having fun matters, and your goal today should be to make it a priority in whatever you do.

December 4

❖ *Don't sell beyond the close.*

The expression "selling beyond the close" is used to describe the habit some people have of continuing to promote an idea after everyone is already on board. Administrators sometimes engage in this activity because they believe that they need to keep people enthusiastic about an idea when later challenges arise. But selling beyond the close is often unproductive. It can make administrators appear to be oblivious of the fact that consensus has already been established or convey the impression that they are

incapable of any other ideas. Even worse, continually trying
to preach to the choir may actually *cause* commitment to
diminish. They may start thinking, "If this idea is so good,
why do they keep promoting it after we said that's what we'd
do? It's almost as though they're trying to talk themselves
into it." For this reason, make a commitment today that
the next time you find yourself on the winning side of a discussion, you'll use that opportunity to start moving ahead,
not continue to persuade those who are already convinced.

December 5

❖ *Learn something new about tenure.*

Few other topics in higher education are as cherished,
controversial, and misunderstood as is tenure. Although
common at North American universities, tenure is less frequently found elsewhere in the world and is often under
attack even at schools where it has long existed. Faculty
members usually view tenure as an essential bulwark of academic freedom. Governing boards often regard tenure as
an expensive luxury and think that it protects the jobs only
of those who perform poorly. The entire issue is highly
complex, but also extremely interesting. Devote a few minutes today to learning something new about the role of
tenure in higher education. You might adopt a historical
perspective and examine when this concept was introduced at colleges and universities, why it was instituted,

and how it has changed over the years. You might adopt a legal perspective and consider the impact of recent case law in clarifying or modifying the traditional view of academic tenure. You might adopt a devil's advocate approach and research arguments used to support positions about tenure that are fundamentally different from your own. Or you might adopt a procedural perspective and explore the policies in place at institutions similar to yours or how institutions without a tenure system protect the academic freedom of their professors. The topic of tenure is so broad that there is certain to be some aspect of it that you will find interesting. Whatever you learn today will be of tremendous value the next time a contentious tenure decision is made on your campus or you are asked to defend your position on this issue.

December 6

❖ *Embrace uncertainty*.

Academic leaders engage in a great deal of planning in order to reduce the amount of uncertainty they have to deal with. But here's the worst-kept secret in higher education: you actually can't plan anything more than a tiny percentage of your institution or program's future even a few years from now. You don't control and can't predict plenty of situations: the precise cycle of a future economic rise or fall, the impact that world events will have on new areas of research, the large transformative gift that a donor suddenly gives you, and so on—and those factors will ultimately shape your program far more than even your most detailed planning. This is not to say that all our planning efforts, whether strategic or annual, are wasted; they're simply not as momentous as we sometimes like to believe. What we're actually doing in all of these activities is not so much planning as *preparing*—putting ourselves in the best possible position to make use of whatever contingencies happen to come our way. In other words, while we can't eliminate uncertainty from our future, we can position our programs to benefit from windfalls and be protected from unforeseen disasters. Remember that not all surprises are unwelcome and that you shouldn't try to control everything about your program. So, make a point today of letting go of the need to plan every detail of what might happen in the future. Embrace the uncertainty you'll inevitably feel when you come to accept that you actually control far less of your future than you thought. That uncertainty is the slack your program needs for increasing its flexibility in the future.

December 7

❖ *Stop being busy.*

Your first thought after being told to stop being so busy may well be, "That's not possible. How can I stop being so busy when there's so much to do? And if I want to be good at my job, there's even much more that I should do!" Certainly, all of us who work in academic administration feel that way. But today's suggestion isn't really about your workload itself. It's about how you approach that workload. That is to say, we're all busy, and some people always seem to be busy just being busy. If we're honest, most of us find ourselves falling into that last category every now and then. Someone asks us how we are or how things are going in our area, and our immediate answer is, "Busy!" without giving the question much thought. That's a bad habit, and it causes us to feel stressed and others to conclude that we may be in over our heads. It's easy to confuse frenetic activity with genuine productivity. But results are judged not by the amount of time or effort we put into them, but by the quality of what we produce by those efforts. For today, stop telling people how busy you are and start answering the question, "How are things going?" in a new way. Say, "I'm getting so much accomplished!" or, even better, identify two or three of the goals you've just achieved. By the end of the day, you'll feel less harried and more in control. You'll feel more accomplished and start conveying to others that you've taken the lead by being in charge of whatever the world might send your way.

December 8

❖ *Notice where the shoe pinches.*

In every job, there are responsibilities that we enjoy a great deal and others that we do only because they're required of us. But we can approach our positions in other

ways as well. We can distinguish the tasks we believe we
do particularly well from those that are less suited to our
talents, inclination, or abilities. Today's suggestion deals
with embracing the negative half of those two perspectives. Look at your performance candidly today, and try
to identify the part of your job that suits you the least or
that you don't do as well as you'd like. Try to think of all
the ways you address or compensate for these disconnects
between you and your responsibilities. Do you tend to
delegate to others tasks that you don't like or think you
don't do particularly well? Do you attempt to do these
tasks anyway, assuming that they go with the territory?
Do you engage in avoidance behavior, putting off unpleasant duties until absolutely necessary and hoping they'll
just go away? And how central are these responsibilities
to what you regard as your most important duties? How
vital to your job would your supervisor or those who report
to you regard these responsibilities? Noticing where the
shoe pinches, in other words, can provide you with insight
into both how you approach your assignment and how
well your current position fits you. As you have seen, no
job ever comes without its share of unpleasant duties, but
a significant mismatch between your strengths or interests, on the one hand, and the most important elements
of your job, on the other, can be a sign that it's time to
consider seriously whether you are in the best possible
position for you.

December 9

❖ *Redouble your efforts.*

As you reflect on the various projects you currently have under way, inevitably one or more will not be proceeding as quickly as you'd like. The goal today is to identify at least one concrete way you can help move that project forward and then follow through on that plan as quickly as possible. Projects sometimes get off to a quick start because of the initial excitement and an enticing ultimate goal. After a while, however, these initiatives can stall because that original burst of enthusiasm fades, the truly difficult work begins, and other priorities, equally pressing, interfere. But if the project is truly important to you, you'll find a way to get it back on track and start making progress again. By redoubling your efforts today, you'll reinforce for others your strong commitment to your goal and prevent your objective from being lost in the flurry of other activities that occur at the end of each term and the calendar year.

December 10

❖ *Think like a student.*

Despite all of the orientation programs and first-year experiences many colleges and universities offer, it's sometimes surprising how little most students understand about the way in which their institution functions. They ask academic deans about financial aid issues, address concerns about their courses to members of the student life staff, and expect their academic advisors to intervene in disputes with their roommates. Perhaps these confusions are not so surprising after all. We deal with matters of institutional hierarchy on a daily basis, but most students have only an occasional need to interact with certain offices. To them, college is simply college, not the labyrinthine arrangement of academic affairs, student affairs, business and finance, community relations, enrollment management, institutional research, and the like that the modern university has become. For this reason, put on the lenses of your students today, and consider how well your program is addressing their needs or answering their questions. Have you made it as clear as possible what you're there to do, which questions are more efficiently handled by other offices, and the range of issues for which you will serve as the students' advocate? Do the people in your program interact with students in a manner that's helpful and friendly but doesn't coddle them or prevent them from developing independent problem-solving skills? If you were a student in your program, what would you regard as your own greatest needs, and have you ever verified those impressions with the students? Is there any action you could take today that would improve the way in which the people who report to you interact with their students?

December 11

❖ *Bookend your day.*

Many of the suggestions in this book require either planning and preparation before a project begins or reflection and analysis when it's completed. Today's suggestion deals with both ends of this process simultaneously. Start the day with a particular goal or intention in mind, and then, just before you leave work, reflect on how much progress you made toward this goal, what worked (or didn't work), and what lessons you can learn from this process. Think of today's exercise as a microcosm of the entire process of intentionality and reflection that you're trying to bring to your administrative work. The goal you choose doesn't have to be anything major. It can even be something intangible like resolving not to get irritated by a person who tends to annoy you. If your style is usually more results oriented, you might prefer to plan on completing a certain proposal before you leave the office today. When you reflect on this exercise afterward, try to examine both what you've learned about the goal or project itself and on how aware of the project you were throughout the day. Did bookending your day cause you to be more mindful of your priorities? If it did, did that mindfulness result in greater productivity, or did it make you tenser, as though something were nagging at you throughout the day? Do you think that having a reflection scheduled at the end of the day caused your work to be of higher quality, more rushed and thus of lower quality, or precisely the same as it would have been otherwise? Do you see other situations in which this type of bookending would be useful?

December 12

❖ *Consider the law of unintended consequences.*

The law of unintended consequences suggests that for any human endeavor, predicting every single result that may follow is impossible. For instance, budgetary conditions may force us to impose a significant increase in tuition and fees, and we may fear that enrollment will decrease because our program is now far more expensive than that of a competitor. Yet we may be surprised to discover that our applicant and enrollment yield actually increases because the higher cost now makes our program seem more "valuable" and prestigious. On the other hand, we may raise faculty and staff salaries anticipating that morale will improve significantly, only to learn that the opposite occurs because of an expectation that increases would be greater than they were; this effort to be generous unexpectedly leads to complaints that if raises are possible now, they could easily have been implemented years earlier. Understanding the law of unintended consequences doesn't mean that administrators should avoid pursuing new endeavors out of concern that something undesirable will result. After all, it is at least as likely that the unintended consequences of any action will be positive as that they'll result in unhappiness or even harm. But being aware that we can't predict every result is a good corrective against feelings of overconfidence or the planning fallacy: the false belief that we can map out our futures with scientific certainty if we plan carefully enough. Unknown factors will always arise, projects will take longer to complete than anticipated, and wise academic leaders will approach new endeavors with a balance of careful preparation and adaptive versatility for when the unexpected occurs.

December 13

❖ *Mix it up.*

Today is for breaking out of old patterns and trying something new. Do something that ordinarily you'd never do. I don't mean something illegal, dangerous, or likely to get you fired, merely something that others wouldn't expect of you. If you're generally a cautious person, take a calculated risk. If you tend to be introverted, get out of your shell. Whatever it is that you personally regard as your wild side, reveal a little bit of it today. Force people to reconsider whatever pigeonhole they've assigned you to by demonstrating that you're far more complex than they thought. Remember that no matter how much others learn about you, there's always a lot more of you that they'll never see. So, mix it up today, and defy other people's expectations.

December 14

❖ *Build flexible time into your schedule.*

You know those people who stick their heads in your doorway and ask, "Got a minute?" They never really want only a minute, do they? In fact, a reliable rule of college administration is that things almost always take longer than people say they will. Sometimes things even take longer that we ourselves expect them to or that they should. One of the reasons that administrative positions become stressful is that we constantly feel as though we're running behind. Today, try to get a handle on everything you have to do by building some flextime into your schedule. If a meeting is supposed to last an hour, block out an hour and a half or two hours. That way, if the meeting runs long, you won't be late for your next appointment or feel harried when you arrive. Even better, if the meeting finishes on time, you'll now have a few moments to catch up on those unexpected tasks that tend to crop up every day. And if you're particularly fortunate and no new fires need to be put out, you'll have time to reflect on your day, make plans for the future, or simply stroll across campus and see how things are going. Remember that administrators don't do their work only in meetings and appointments. Academic leadership involves much more than simply crossing off items on a list. If you get into the habit of building flexible time into your schedule, you'll not just be a more relaxed academic leader; you'll be a more effective one.

December 15

※ *Remember that you're a symbol.*

As soon as you accept an administrative position, you stop being simply "Dr. Jones, professor of European intellectual history," and start also being "the dean" (or chair or provost or president or whatever title you happen to hold). In other words, you don't stop being who you are, but you assume an important new symbolic function. People who may have felt free to share their views with you as their colleague might be not quite as candid now as they'd been before. Alternatively, you may discover that you've become a lightning rod for anger, suspicion, and jealousy. You may regard yourself as perfectly collegial and accessible, only to find that you are treated as "the enemy." As we saw back on September 17, that rancor isn't really about you. Just as part of someone's reaction to you could result from whatever's going on in that person's life that you couldn't possibly control, so can part of someone's treatment of you be due to what you symbolize, not who you are. It's common for people to both grumble about and fear the boss, no matter who the boss is. But they also turn to the boss for answers and resources, even in the midst of a severe budget crisis or a situation far beyond the supervisor's control. Members of the faculty and staff frequently project their own hopes, fears, and meanings onto their academic leaders. It goes with the territory, as they say. So, as problems or challenges arise today, reflect on the way in which your function as a symbol changes the nature of these situations and makes your role either easier or more complicated.

December 16

❖ *Identify your favorite word.*

If you listen to a number of speeches by any politician, you're likely to notice certain words being used more frequently than you hear when other political figures speak. That's because we all have our favorite words, and we tend to rely on them over and over again. What's your favorite word? Is there some term that other people say you tend to overuse? Or is there a word that has a sound you find particularly attractive or a connotation that gives you an especially positive feeling? Give some consideration to that word today. Ask yourself why you regard that particular word as so attractive or important to you. What does it suggest about your values or your individual perspectives? Once you're aware of your own favorite word, you can begin to be more strategic about its use. That is, you can stop overusing it and start adopting it more effectively as an element of a consistent message about your goals for the future.

December 17

❖ *Simplify your focus.*

Some of our goals are hard to obtain because we're pulled in so many directions at once. We feel that we're spread so thin with personnel issues, curriculum development, institutional advancement, faculty and student problems, assessment, strategic planning, our supervisor's own vision for our program, our personal career goals, and all the other concerns of our daily lives that nothing is getting the attention it deserves. For at least a little while today, try to simplify your focus and concentrate on the single most important goal you have among this entire range of competing concerns. In other words, if you could—or if you had to—devote your attention to only one concern or aspect of your life from this point forward, what would it be? Why is that particular area of your life or career so much more important to you than all the others? By keeping your focus simple, you can prevent yourself from getting distracted by all the less significant demands for your time that will inevitably come your way. In fact, if it's possible, jettison a few of your low-priority distractions in order to give yourself more time to concentrate on what really matters. Otherwise you could end up getting a lot of things done but never achieving anything that really matters.

December 18

❖ *Support those who support you.*

Too often in higher education, responsibility and authority don't go hand in hand. While that statement applies to many people who work in higher education, it has particular relevance to the support staff. These are frequently members of our administrative teams who have the word *assistant* or *associate* in their titles. We assign tasks to the assistant chair, associate dean, and executive assistant to the president that place them in difficult situations. They're dependent for their success on people who don't report to them and over whom they have no real authority. If someone withholds information, misses a deadline, or performs a task unacceptably, the member of the support staff will be unable to do his or her job properly but will have little recourse (except to come squealing to you) to remedy the situation. Because of the challenging nature of their jobs, you can support your staff by making it clear to everyone that when any member of your team makes a request or imposes a deadline, that person is speaking with your voice and in your name. By protecting the interests of your support staff, you'll help make their jobs easier. Perhaps of equal importance, you'll find that you get more work accomplished as a result.

December 19

❖ *Identify your brand.*

Today, focus on the unique (or at least distinctive) elements of your personal brand. Notice that I'm not talking today about your program or institution. They also have their own brands or identities, and while being able to define these distinctive characteristics clearly is very useful, it's not the main purpose of today's suggestion. The focus for this exercise is your own identity as a scholar and administrator—the things that make you who you are. Think, for instance, of those aspects of your style, personality, and approach that make you particularly well suited for your work. What do you want to be remembered for after you leave your current position? If you were asked to create a personal motto that summarized your values, what would it be? What does your institution gain from having you in your current administrative position that it probably wouldn't receive if someone else had this job? All of these reflections help you identify the value that you add to your work—your contributions that go far beyond the attainment of daily goals or the pursuit of a long-term plan. They help you identify the key elements of your administrative philosophy and keep that philosophy in the foreground of your thoughts as you perform today's responsibilities.

December 20

❧ *Write an article on academic administration.*

You didn't reach your current position without having learned something important about how colleges and universities are run. So today's the day to begin sharing that insight with others. Numerous excellent publications deal with issues of concern to academic administrators at all levels. Among the publications you may already read are the *Department Chair* and *Dean and Provost* (both published by Jossey-Bass), *The Academic Leader*, *Recruitment and Retention*, and *Student Affairs Leader* (all published by Magna Publications), *Community College Review* and the electronic journal *Active Learning in Higher Education* (both distributed by Sage), and *Change* magazine (published by the Taylor & Francis Group). All of these newsletters, magazines, and journals are constantly looking for authors with practical insights to share. The articles published by these journals range widely in length, so don't feel that you have nothing to offer if you don't have time to produce a twenty-page manuscript. For certain venues, a three- or four-page note or essay will be perfect, and you could easily write that article a paragraph at a time between meetings today. Writing down your thoughts will help you to focus them better, even for your own use. In addition, you'll be doing an important service for other administrators who face many of the same challenges that you do. You could even begin to establish an international reputation as an expert in some aspect of higher education administration. So spend some time today looking at the publication guidelines of journals dealing with academic administration and begin writing your own contribution.

December 21

❖ *Explain the system.*

Academic leaders understand how colleges and universities work because they studied in them for many years, made them their career, and spend most of their days employed by them. But students (who may be relatively new to this experience) and external constituents (whose sole familiarity with higher education may have come when they were students themselves many years ago) frequently have a limited understanding of how these institutions operate. They may believe that if they have an idea for a course that they think is interesting, you can simply offer it. Or they may know someone "who'd make a really great professor" and assume you'll want to offer that person a full-time job. It's easy to scoff at these misconceptions, but consider all the false conclusions you'd certainly draw if you were suddenly dropped into that person's world. When we don't know how an institution works, we assume

124

it functions like the institutions we already know. So a goal today is to explain a bit about how your college or university functions to a person who is probably unfamiliar with it. Don't talk down to the person, but clarify processes and procedures to someone who may well need this information. For instance, you might describe how curriculum proposals are developed and approved or how faculty searches are conducted. You may well end the day with a better understanding of the process yourself by having had to explain and justify it to someone who doesn't share your basic assumptions.

December 22

❖ *Associate with someone you admire.*

Just as we try to serve as positive role models for our own students and faculty members, so can we benefit from the example set by our own mentor or hero. If you were to select someone you particularly admire, who would it be? Try to identify a person who's not so remote from your world that you'd never have a reasonable chance of meeting him or her. Rather than an international leader whose name everyone recognizes instantly, identify someone who has made a significant contribution to your academic discipline, in the field of higher education administration, or at your own institution. Then see if you can find a way of getting to know this person a bit better in order to benefit from his or her positive example. I'm certainly not recommending that you act like a stalker or continually thrust yourself into the presence of someone who would clearly rather be left alone. But most people, even those who have attained a relatively high position in their fields, are more accessible than you may think and are willing to give advice to people who sincerely want it. (Besides, think of how flattering it would be to be asked to serve as a role model or mentor.) Just be sure to respect the other person's time and accept only as much contact as he or she seems willing to give. You might make an initial contact through an e-mail, letter, or casual meeting at a conference. Mention why you admire what that person has done, and then ask a fairly specific question that relates closely to his or her area of expertise. Follow up with a warm expression of gratitude, and see if the relationship continues from that point. It may well be only the beginning.

December 23

❖ *Have a meeting standing up.*

As we've had numerous occasions to observe, there are all types of meetings in higher education. Sometimes we need to get people together in order to share ideas, bond as a unit, or accomplish a goal that can't be achieved in any other way. At other times, the specific task you want to accomplish may take precedence over team building, and efficiency may be a higher priority than developing relationships. But the next time you're in charge of one of these very task-oriented meetings, arrange it in such a way that all the participants are required to stand the entire time. While you'll certainly want to be mindful of any participant whose health or physical challenges make it difficult to stand for an extended time, meetings where people can't get too settled in tend to be marvels of efficiency. Schedule your session for a location where there are no chairs, or move all the seats out of the room. Start by describing the task your group is going to complete, and make it clear that you intend to continue the meeting until a successful conclusion is reached. People have a disincentive to prolong the discussion by pontificating, repeating points that have already been made, and talking for the sheer pleasure of hearing their own voices. If you start conducting all your meetings this way, you'll lose the opportunity to explore different perspectives in a more leisurely or comprehensive manner, and you may begin noticing that your staff will become more fragmented. But for purely result-oriented meetings, conducting them with all participants on their feet can save you a great deal of time.

December 24

❖ *Trust your instincts.*

As academics, we love to analyze things. But we sometimes let our talent at analyzing situations get in the way of our ability to discern a simpler, more underlying truth. Today, see if you draw conclusions just as well (or perhaps even better) by trusting your instincts as you do by carefully critiquing each situation. There are times, after all, when we all simply need to go with our gut reactions. In your own work, there may be certain people who make you feel uncomfortable, even though you can't identify the reason. (Someday you may well learn that your instincts were quite correct.) Or there may be a new opportunity that everyone feels is perfect for you but for which you sense some inner reluctance. Spend some time today listening to your inner voice and giving it the benefit of the doubt. It may not be a completely reliable guide in every situation—that's why those analytical skills will never cease to be important—but it can be surprisingly useful in the vast majority of cases. The good administrator knows *how* to take full advantage of both instinct and reasoning. The wise administrator knows *when* to use each.

December 25

❖ *Take a day completely off.*

Higher education administration is a job that requires you to be on duty pretty much 24/7. In fact, the higher you go up the administrative ladder, the more demanding your schedule will be. But this general pattern doesn't mean that you should never take time for yourself. Today is one of those days. Take the day completely off, and don't even think of your professional responsibilities. Don't check your e-mail. Don't review any upcoming deadlines. Don't worry about what may go wrong or who may need to get in touch with you. Shut off your cell phone if at all possible. Spend your day instead simply enjoying the company of the most important people in your life. Carve out a little time for yourself, reading a book that has nothing to do with your job (in fact, put this book down just as soon as you complete this paragraph), going for a walk, or taking a nap. Devote yourself to thinking about things that have as little as possible to do with your leadership responsibilities. Revel in the joy of having at least one entire day when you can set your professional responsibilities completely behind you.

December 26

❖ *Make a wish.*

Throughout the year, you spend your days engaging in planning and preparation. But today's the day to take a completely different approach to the future: make a wish about something that relates to your program, career, or personal goals. Certainly it can be important to be practical and realistic about objectives, but that's not the object of today's suggestion. Today is all about dreams, and the assignment is for you to dream big. Think of that chance occurrence that would positively transform your program into something utterly distinctive from all its competitors. Or envision the job that would give you the greatest amount of satisfaction. Or imagine obtaining some other goal in your life that you regard as singularly important and fulfilling. Then spend a moment or two wishing that what you've envisioned might come true. And that's it. Today's thought experiment is not about making detailed plans or developing all the strategies you'd need to fulfill those plans. It's simply about identifying what you desire in life and then wishing that you'll receive it. Keep in mind the proverb that if wishes were horses, beggars would ride. But also keep in mind one other proverb: Be careful what you wish for; you just may get it.

December 27

❖ *Count your blessings.*

It's easy to become fixated on negative aspects of higher education. Budgets are never sufficient to do everything we want. Processes are often cumbersome. Sometimes we seem to be surrounded by people whose sole job is to create problems for us. But that picture is actually misleading. As academic leaders, we have incredible opportunities to work with interesting ideas, improve people's lives, and achieve goals that make the world a better place. So, spend some time today identifying all the good things that are going on in your world and the positive aspects of your job. Don't stop until you have a list of at least ten excellent reasons why you should be proud of what you do. You can include personal achievements, aspects related to your official position, characteristics of the colleagues you're fortunate enough to work with, distinctive features of your institution, or anything else you like. If you take this suggestion seriously, you're likely to end up with a list containing far more than ten items.

December 28

✢ *Reflect on your achievements.*

As the calendar year draws to a close, it's a good time to conduct a self-assessment of how well you've been progressing toward your goals. What are your accomplishments over the past twelve months? What goals did you think you'd achieve but you weren't able to complete? Feel free to take some well-earned pride when you look at everything you've accomplished. Too often we complete one task and then immediately proceed to the next one without even pausing to congratulate ourselves on how successfully we've completed our work. And if there are significant goals that you thought you'd achieve this year but weren't able to reach, don't waste time in regret or blaming yourself. Simply consider which goals are worth carrying over to the next year and what you might do to reach a more successful outcome in the future. (If the goals

131

are not worth carrying over to next year, were they really that important to you to begin with?) End this activity by feeling good once more about the achievements you do have. As frustrating as our jobs can be at times, we do complete a lot of very important work, and you should end this year with a positive feeling about all the contributions you've made.

December 29

⁜ *Share credit.*

Think of your most recent achievement—that special accomplishment in which you take particular pride. Now think of all the other people who made that achievement possible. Even if you're accustomed to thinking, "I did it all by myself," there's undoubtedly at least one other person who helped you along the way. You may have secured a major financial gift for your institution with no assistance from anyone else—but it was really the donor or foundation that provided the money. You may have published a stunning groundbreaking book in your field with absolutely no assistance from any other researcher—but your publisher was still instrumental in transforming your manuscript into a widely available book. Most of the great things that we do as academic administrators make it quite easy to identify others whose contributions were essential. We worked with a committee, were assisted by a collaborator, benefited from the help of a fine office staff, or were aided in countless other ways by our colleagues. Make a special effort today to acknowledge the help you received in completing your significant achievement. Share credit with others, and make sure that they understand the degree to which this achievement was theirs too.

December 30

❖ *Identify the first major task you'd like to tackle in the new year.*

As the year ends, reflect on your successes and achievements. In fact, that's precisely what I encouraged you to do only two days ago. But don't spend all your time patting yourself on the back. Your work's not over yet. A new year is ahead, with plenty of opportunities and challenges to face during the coming term. So while it's still quiet and you have some time to catch your breath, think about the first major hurdle you'd like to jump over on January 1. Choose something big enough and important enough that you'll look back on it a year from now and feel that all your effort was worthwhile. Devote a few minutes today to deciding what your strategy will be. Then as soon as the new year begins, you'll find yourself ready to hit the ground running.

December 31

❧ *Consider why students leave.*

Some students decide that our program or institution is not for them. That decision is only natural, since we all make decisions every day about which choices truly suit our needs, goals, and personalities. Student attrition can be particularly troubling, however, if it occurs at a higher rate for you than for your peers or if your school is heavily tuition driven and thus being deprived of an important source of revenue. Yet regardless of whether your rate of attrition is large or small, reflect on why students may be leaving your program or institution. One of the best ways to accomplish this task is to turn the entire question on its head and ask why students stay. What are the factors that cause students to remain eager about pursuing the opportunities that you offer, work hard to meet the challenges posed, and develop the skills that will allow them to succeed? Sometimes attrition is caused by a poor match between the goals of the program and the expectations of the students entering it. See if you can think of at least one better way to explain your mission to potential students or to help those who could truly benefit from the excellent curriculum that you provide succeed.

January

January 1

❖ *Do an anonymous good deed.*

Start the year by performing an act of generosity that the recipient will never be able to trace back to you. Anonymous good deeds can accomplish a great deal in improving the general morale in your area and keeping the workplace a positive, energy-filled environment. The message you'll be sending to members of your faculty and staff is that they work in an environment where people truly care for one another, look out for each other's interests without regard for personal benefit, and notice what other members of the community need, want, or can use. When people feel supported, they're more likely to relax and do their work in a manner that allows their creativity to emerge. In addition, anonymous generosity is satisfying in a way that no expression of gratitude can ever be. By following today's suggestion, you'll have an opportunity to think about what your coworkers need or enjoy, and that knowledge will help make you more sensitive and effective as a supervisor.

January 2

❖ *Create a leadership journal.*

One of the best ways to become more intentional about your growth as an administrator is to keep a leadership journal. In this journal, you reflect periodically on your administrative philosophy, track the decisions you've made and the initiatives you've planned, and evaluate what has been effective and what hasn't been successful. You can use your journal to keep track of your ideas and hopes for the future at the same time that it helps you make sense of the present. A leadership journal can take the form of an electronic blog, a simple word processing file, or the familiar bound volume. It's not important to enter something in your journal every day, as long as you do it on a regular basis. But however often you decide to make an entry, incorporate the journal into your regular routine. Schedule time for it on your calendar if necessary. Within a few months, you'll find that it helps you take better advantage of the opportunities that come to every academic administrator.

January 3

❖ *Thank someone.*

At every college or university, there are plenty of people whose quality of work far exceeds the compensation they receive. Make a special effort today to identify one of these people and express your gratitude in a meaningful way. Don't just write a quick note that says, "Thank you for all you've done," or jot down a few platitudes. Be specific about why you are grateful to this person. Mention at least one important contribution the person has made for which you'll always be grateful. Talk about the impact his or her work has had; perhaps it made everyone else feel good, reduced costs, or improved your program's effectiveness. Make it clear that your institution is a better place because of this employee. If possible, express your gratitude in person. Go wherever that person works and deliver your message in person. If that isn't possible, craft a handwritten note, making it personal enough that the recipient will know you took the time to notice all the contributions others have simply ignored.

January 4

❖ *Document your successes.*

Much of what we accomplish as academic administrators remains intangible. Our budget proposals, curricular reforms, and policy reviews usually don't result in the same kind of instant satisfaction that can be felt when a publication has been accepted, a grant proposal has been funded, or a student finally understands a concept that had long been puzzling. For this reason, it can be particularly important for administrators to document the nature of their successes and reflect on how they've made a difference. Create a file folder in which you can keep printed materials and a computer folder for electronic documents, and begin storing items related to your achievements. What would not be the same at your college or university if it were not for you? How many new positions did you create or, in times of budget cuts, how many jobs did you save? How has research been enhanced or learning enriched through your policies? Whenever you set aside documents related to your activities, include a note about why that initiative was important. Be selective. Don't simply include every document that you created; rather, choose only those related to your best achievements. This portfolio of successes will soon become invaluable to you. You can review it whenever things are not going well or you sense that your contributions have been ineffective. You can refer to it for examples during an annual review or when applying for another position. And you can study it for what it reveals about your own best practices whenever you face a challenging situation you haven't encountered before.

January 5

❖ *Stop procrastinating.*

Every administrative position has enjoyable duties, as well as activities that are substantially less pleasant. Many of our least desirable tasks involve confrontation or difficult personnel issues: the employee who must be let go, the student or researcher who has been accused of academic misconduct, the overly strident colleague who tries our patience, and so on. For some administrators, particular types of responsibilities, such as preparing long reports or making public presentations, are the real annoyances. But no matter which part of our jobs we enjoy least, there will always be one task—or perhaps one type of task—that we end up putting off longer than we should. Today's suggestion is to choose one of these lingering responsibilities and resolve to address it as soon as possible. In most cases, we find that the activity we've been avoiding is not nearly as unpleasant as we had feared. Yet even when the work proves distasteful, we end up with the satisfaction of getting it behind us. After all, college administration is not about making the easy or popular decisions; it's about making the right decisions for the good of those we serve. Similarly, as academic leaders, we don't have the luxury of taking on only the tasks we enjoy. We must often do something unpleasant because it is in the best interests of our institution and the people who work, study, and conduct research under our supervision. And looking out for their best interests is our most important responsibility.

January 6

❖ *Listen to an opposing view.*

The strength of higher education doesn't derive from a uniformity of outlook or opinion. It's found in the diversity of views, methods, and intellectual approaches that we encounter across disciplines, academic units, and entire institutions. We benefit from defending our perspectives to others when we're justified and from modifying our views when new evidence or argumentation warrants a reappraisal. In our administrative responsibilities as in our academic pursuits, often multiple paths lead to a common goal. Even more important, there are also multiple goals that may be appropriate at a particular stage in an institution's development. Today, therefore, identify someone whose perceptions are distinctly different from your own. Talk with this person constructively about his or her point of view. Your goal for this activity is not to persuade the other person to change his or her mind but rather to understand more completely this person's perspectives and priorities. Don't resort to argument or debate. Don't even spend a great deal of time defending your own point of view. Rather, use the conversation as an opportunity to gain insight into a different way of looking at a situation. You may well find that even if your own views remain the same, they become more nuanced, complex, or balanced because of this exchange.

January 7

❖ *Learn something new about assessment.*

Even if you're the assessment guru at your school, there's always something more you can learn about assessment techniques and how they can be used to improve the quality of education or the programs you supervise. Books and Web sites devoted to new approaches to assessment appear all the time, and these resources can help both the individual professor who wants to enhance student learning in a specific course and the program director who wants his or her graduates to become more innovative in their research. If you feel you've already mastered everything you need to know about assessment in your own area of specialty, try to learn the latest approaches to assessment in a different area, such as in general education programs. Or if you're an expert in assessing undergraduate programs, learn more about how assessment works in graduate school, even if you're unlikely to have responsibilities in this area. Finally, if you already know everything there is to know about assessing academic programs, find out more about assessment strategies as they apply to student life programs, the business office, alumni relations, athletics, and other aspects of college life. You'll discover that the more you know about this topic, the more there is to learn. And what you discover today will inevitably lead to more creative ideas about the continual improvement of your own programs.

January 8

❖ *Reread a favorite book.*

Returning to a book that we enjoyed long ago can provide us with surprising insights. Sometimes we're instantly carried back to an earlier time in our lives and reminded of ideas and emotions that we've somehow lost track of. At other times we discover that we've changed so much since we first read the book that we can barely remember why we enjoyed it then. In either case, however, the rereading becomes tremendously important. It reinforces both who we are now and where we came from. It reminds us that we're on a professional journey with many stops still along the way. Perhaps several years from now you'll reread your current favorite book and have a completely different reaction to it. Use today's activity to recognize the ways that you have changed, as well as the ways in which you've remained the same person as your life and career have progressed. Value both your growth and your background that made that growth possible. If no other benefit comes from today's experience, you'll find that it's a way of reconnecting with an earlier version of yourself.

January 9

❖ *Pay a visit.*

Even if you're the type of administrator who follows the philosophy of management by walking around, there are likely to be places on your campus that you don't visit often. Make it a priority today to travel to one of these locations. Unless you are the chief executive officer of your institution, you might even consider visiting a unit that doesn't report to you at all. Administrators in academic affairs can learn a great deal from touring the residence halls. Student life personnel can gain new insights from viewing research facilities. Supervisors in the business office can benefit from sitting in on a class or two. You may discover that a visit to an office that you don't know well tells you things about your college or university that you would never have expected. Introduce yourself to any employees you haven't yet met and find out more about who they are and what their responsibilities include. No matter which office you end up visiting, you'll encounter something that will help you do your own job better.

January 10

❖ *Discover time puddles.*

Time puddles are those little periods of time that seem too brief to do anything useful and often simply go to waste. They're the five or ten minutes you spend waiting for a telephone call to come in, a meeting to start, or an office to open. Usually we fritter away these opportunities by assuming that nothing productive can be done in such a short time. But assemble enough time puddles through a week or month, and you can end up with a good-sized lake (or at least a fairly large pond) of available time. Keep a list of activities that are important to you and devote the few minutes of your next time puddle to one of them. You certainly can't get an article written in only five or ten minutes, but you could identify a few resources for it through your library's database. You can't conduct a whole meeting in that time, but you can draft a brief note of thanks to a donor or a get-well card for a staff member. You can't complete an entire grant application, but you can research a deadline, make an appointment with a program officer so that you can have a more detailed discussion, or download an application. Once you get in the habit of using these time puddles for appropriate but important tasks, it can be surprising just how much you can accomplish during periods that might otherwise have been wasted. Much of this book, in fact, was written by taking advantage of time puddles in precisely this way.

January 11

❖ *Continue reinventing yourself.*

Over the course of our lives, we have the opportunity to become many different people: child, student, adult, lover, spouse, parent, and so on. In a similar way, over the course of our professional careers, we are likely to assume a number of different roles as our assignments change and our responsibilities grow. But even in the midst of all these constantly changing roles, we have a chance to reinvent ourselves in other ways. Faced with one situation, we may become advocates of change, while at other times we may defend the current order because we believe that certain changes are unwarranted or unwise. In one stage of our lives, we may derive a great deal of satisfaction from a particular element of our work that a few years later we come to regard as boring or unchallenging. Conscious of how you can change as an academic leader, reflect today on the evolving roles you've played throughout your administrative life, and imagine how reinventing yourself yet again would best serve the needs of your institution. For instance, you may decide that what your program needs next is an expert in an emerging type of technology. You could decide that you'll endeavor to become a bit more tolerant of those who try your patience or that you need to liberate your schedule from unproductive commitments. Perhaps you'll conclude that what you really need is a more radical reinvention—something that requires extensive retraining or a completely different career path. Just remember that whichever path you choose, constructive reinvention can benefit both you and your institution. Besides, a certain degree of development is inevitable, so why not be completely intentional about it?

January 12

❖ *Improve one policy.*

Unless you participated in the founding of your institution, you probably inherited a large number of policies that you didn't create. Most of these policies probably work reasonably well, although others are likely to be cumbersome, ill conceived, or counterproductive. It may well seem overwhelming to consider revising all of the policies and procedures that need updating. So don't get caught up in the feeling that you have to change them all; today, decide that you're simply going to change one of them. Select a policy that seems to be causing the most difficulty for the area you supervise or that's not producing the results you need. Dedicate your energies today to improving this one small corner of your institution. Over time, incremental changes like the one you're initiating can result in huge improvements. But from the start, you'll derive a sense of satisfaction from having made a change for the better. Recall precisely what this satisfaction feels like as you proceed to the other challenges you face throughout your academic year. Although certain actions may yield results only in the longer term, if you approach each situation with the same desire to do what is right for your institution, significant benefits will ultimately occur. But that will start only if you commit yourself to making that single small improvement today.

January 13

❖ *Find a way to say yes to someone.*

At times, being an administrator can seem like an endless series of meetings in which you have to disappoint people. Financial considerations, established policies, and the long-term good of your institution can mean that you will never be able to approve every request for a raise, office upgrade, promotion, program modification, or adjustment of responsibilities that is requested of you. Not only can working with restraints of this sort cause members of the faculty and staff to begin seeing all administrators as obstacles to progress, but it can also affect the way that we tend to view ourselves and our responsibilities. As an antidote to this situation, find a way today to say yes to someone about something. You may not be in a position to make anyone's lifelong dream come true, but you can help a member of your faculty or staff in some small way and gain your own sense of satisfaction as a result. Good administrators understand that *NO* may often be the best answer to many questions, but it should never become their default position. There are many times when we as academic leaders can encourage creativity and strengthen institutional support simply by giving our blessing to the initiative or proposal of someone who makes a well-considered request. Look for one of these opportunities today to help make a good idea become reality.

January 14

⁘ *Talk about research.*

Every member of the faculty, regardless of the nature of his or her specific assignment, is continually engaging in some form of research, scholarship, or creative activity.

For some positions, this activity may consist of little more than keeping up with new developments in the field, while for others, research may be the only responsibility that's assigned. We tend to celebrate achievements in scholarship during annual reviews and, even more formally, during evaluations for promotion, tenure, or post-tenure review. Yet although most faculty members are justifiably proud of their scholarly endeavors and devote considerable effort to them, few people outside their disciplines ask about their progress in research on a regular basis. But talking to a faculty member about his or her current research, particularly if you do not know that person well, can be valuable in several ways. As a start, it can reinforce for others just how much you appreciate the creative talent that exists at your college or university. Second, it provides a natural ice-breaker for a conversation that can then lead into other areas. Third, most people enjoy knowing that someone is interested in what they do and take their work seriously enough to ask about it. For all of these reasons, take a moment today to talk to a faculty member about whom you may know very little and ask a few questions about his or her current scholarly projects. Make it clear that the purpose of the conversation is not to check up on anyone; you are simply interested in a topic that matters so much to the faculty member involved.

January 15

❖ *Balance your life.*

Good administrators keep matters in perspective and their lives in balance. Workaholics or those who feel that they're married to their jobs may feel that they're being particularly productive, but they're really deceiving themselves and others. With this thought in mind, reflect on the various spheres of your life (work, family, friends, causes that you believe in, and the like), and try to see whether any of them has grown too far out of proportion or, at the other extreme, shrunk to insignificance. Be dedicated to your job, certainly, but make sure that all other aspects of who you are receive the proper amount of attention as well. Make time for your family, friends, and personal life. Get enough exercise. Determine whether your actions are being guided by your cherished values and core beliefs. Take time to relax. Be aware if you're becoming stressed, depressed, or anxious. Keep your workload manageable. Direct your anger only in appropriate ways. While many of these suggestions may seem to have little to do with your role as an administrator, you won't remain very effective as an academic leader without them.

January 16

❖ *Set your priorities.*

Ask most administrators, and they'll identify their highest administrative priority without even a pause to think. At least, they can identify what they always *declare* to be their highest priority. But sometimes the goals we announce and the goals we truly believe in are not precisely the same. So today, reflect on your priorities with absolute candor. If you could achieve any administrative goal whatsoever, what would it be? Consider this question without regard for what other people may expect you to say, the policies and stated mission of your institution, or what your supervisor or board believes your highest priorities ought to be. From your own perspective, if you could change or accomplish only one thing, what would it be? Suppose that you were given absolutely free rein to accomplish a single task. What would your goals be? As you consider these questions, you might modify your public statements in such a way that they more closely reflect your basic values. Or you may realize that although external forces make it necessary for you to follow an agenda that others have set, you can continue to work independently and discreetly to achieve the goals that you regard as more meaningful. In either case, it's important to take time to reflect on whether your public persona has become too far removed from your personal convictions and, if they have, what actions you should take as a result.

152

January 17

❖ *Let a student gush.*

It can be all too easy for academic administrators to get caught up in negativity. After all, people bring you their problems all day long. You hear complaint after complaint. You often have to deal with people who fail to honor their commitments. After hearing such distressing news day after day, week after week, nearly anyone would be cynical. Why don't people ever think of coming to an administrator with good news? Well, today go looking for some. When a student comes to see you about any issue whatsoever, extend that visit a few minutes by asking about that student's favorite professor. If the nature of your position is such that you don't have much contact with students, get out of your office, go to where the students are, and engage one of them in a conversation about the best educational experience he or she has had. You may well find this practice so valuable that you make it part of your regular routine. It can provide you with insights that entire stacks of course evaluations will never give you. Moreover, if you continue having conversations of this sort, you'll quickly learn who the best professors in your program are and, more important, why they're outstanding. Finally, whenever it makes your day to hear a student say something wonderful about a faculty member, make someone else's day too: share what you've learned with that professor.

153

January 18

❧ *Attack your ignorance.*

Specialization may well be the greatest strength and most severe weakness of higher education today. By becoming experts in a field, we're able to conduct research that leads to new discoveries, insights, or applications. We expose our students to the latest developments in our disciplines and train them to recognize claims that have been disproven or lines of inquiry that have been abandoned as unfruitful. Certainly no one can attain a truly deep level of knowledge in every field simultaneously. And yet the type of extreme specialization found on most university campuses tends to narrow our focus and blind us to the connections that are possible between our disciplines and others. If we teach undergraduate students, we may find ourselves cut off from the experience of our own students who are even now broadening their horizons through general education courses. As a result, everyone in higher education periodically needs to explore a field that he or she understands very little. So, today's suggestion is to choose the academic field about which you know the least—even if it's a subject that you dislike or disdain—and make a sincere effort to learn more about it by reading at least one important work in that field. In most cases, you'll discover connections you never knew existed between that field and your own, and your teaching, research, and administrative acumen will all improve as a result.

January 19

❖ *Demonstrate good stewardship.*

For every college or university, as well as every program within institutions, there are people in the community who feel an affiliation to it. Often these supporters are donors, but they could just as easily be the people who attend lectures, concerts, public discussions, or art openings. They may have given large financial gifts in the past or offered their time as volunteers to or participants in certain events. Today select one of these supporters, and write a brief note of appreciation. If the person is already a contributor, your note will provide good stewardship of the gift you've received, probably encourage similar gifts in the future, and make the donor feel that his or her generosity was appreciated. The expression of thanks will be all the more meaningful to the donor because it isn't tied to any particular occasion or an additional solicitation. Moreover, if the person hasn't yet contributed funding to your program, your thoughtful note may encourage a gift in the future, at the same time that it indicates just how much you value the support you've already received.

January 20

❖ Review your institution's mission statement.

Undoubtedly you've read your school's mission statement. You may have even written it. But it's time well spent to reread it occasionally. So much of what we do as administrators forces us to spend our days "in the weeds" that we may lose that larger sense of why we became academic leaders in the first place. If your institution's mission statement is particularly well written, it won't confine itself to platitudes about excellence in teaching, scholarship, and service to the region. Instead, it will enunciate a clear vision about what makes the school unique, why it exists when there are plenty of other colleges and universities, and where the institution may be heading. (If your institution's mission statement doesn't meet this standard, it may be time for that document to be revisited.) A good mission statement reminds you why, on even your most challenging days, you keep on trying. At least once a year, all administrators need to reread the mission statement that supposedly guides their actions and decisions, and then consider whether they're actually fulfilling the mission that it describes.

January 21

❖ *Expand your resources.*

Institutions sometimes receive grants because a research project is conceived (or perhaps already well under way), and then likely possibilities for external funding are identified. But it's also not uncommon for someone at a college or university to notice that foundations or government agencies are funding work in a particular area and think, "We could do *that*." The nature of external funding is that opportunities change all the time as needs evolve and the interests of donors shift. For this reason, it can be fruitful every now and then for academic leaders to revisit the major sources of external support and determine which types of projects are being funded now. Every week the *Chronicle of Higher Education* lists funding deadlines in its Gazette section, a resource that can also be searched online through the journal's Web site (http://chronicle.com/gazette/). Another major clearinghouse of grant opportunities is available at grants.gov, a Web site managed by the Department of Health and Human Services. Several states post databases of funding opportunities that are available in their regions, and individual disciplines sometimes distribute information about grants available to scholars in that field. Finally, some excellent institutional sources are available, including a Web site created by the Office of Proposal Development at Texas A&M University (http://opd.tamu.edu/funding-opportunities/), which categorizes resources that are available by discipline, academic level (such as undergraduate research versus postdoctoral fellowships), and special emphasis (such as programs to enhance diversity). Scan one or more of these lists to find a funding source related to the disciplines you supervise.

January 22

❖ *Dare to dream.*

With all of the day-to-day challenges that administrators face, it can be easy to get caught up in routine issues and find that you have no energy left for the issues that really matter. Today, spend a few minutes dreaming about what is best, not merely about what is attainable. If your institution or program were to be transformed into something truly remarkable, what would the result be? If funding were unlimited, how would you take the strengths that already exist in your program and extend them to achieve their full potential? How would you eliminate any challenges, threats, or weaknesses that you face? What do you regard as the ideal environment for work, learning, and discovery in your disciplines? Even if that absolutely perfect image never comes about, are there any aspects of it that you can begin moving toward today? Dreams are not without value. You can use them to guide you in ways that you may not have considered if you felt compelled to examine only what's immediately practical.

158

January 23

❖ *Focus on your lowest priorities.*

As academic leaders, we spend a great deal of time paying attention to our highest priorities and making sure that we have a clear vision for them. In fact, only a week ago, that suggestion appeared in this guide: set your priorities. But what do we do about the things that we regard as our lowest administrative priorities? Every now and then, we need to spend some time thinking about those objectives as well. For one thing, doing so can help us spot activities that demand too much unproductive time; if we can eliminate these low-priority tasks altogether, we can free ourselves up for pursuits that we consider far more important. In addition, reflecting on our lowest administrative priorities can tell us something about ourselves and our values. Do any of them involve tasks that those around us—for instance, our supervisors, peers, and employees—regard as more important than we do? Where does this difference in perception arise? Most important, are there ways in which these other views may be right? Have we given too little emphasis to a task that's vital to our position and our institutions? Keeping your mind open in this way, identify your lowest administrative priorities today, and ask yourself what they reveal about your core values that causes you to think they're relatively unimportant.

January 24

❖ Get back in touch with someone who made a difference.

The single most important goal in higher education is to improve people's lives. It's ironic, therefore, that many of us who have benefited the most from what colleges and universities can offer fall out of touch with the very teachers and mentors who meant most to us. Remedy this oversight today. Send an appreciative note to someone who was instrumental in helping you attain your current success. If you'd be more comfortable doing so, reach your mentor by telephone, or stop by to say hello in person. Don't let this opportunity to express your gratitude slip away.

January 25

❖ Share a meal.

The thirty-thousand-foot view that administrators develop at their institutions can be a blessing and a curse. On the one hand, it helps academic leaders to see every issue in its entirety and to become aware of implications that others tend to overlook. On the other hand, being too far up the chain of command makes it all too easy to become cut off from how decisions and policies affect the daily lives of students, faculty members, and the staff.

Today, have a meal in one of the dining halls at your school. If you're at an institution that doesn't have dining halls, a local fast food restaurant where students and faculty members gather will serve a similar purpose. Don't sit down with a group of people you already know or sit at an empty table, hoping that others will eventually join you. Try to join a group of students you've never met before, explain that you want to talk about whatever's on their minds, ask a few questions, and be sure that you are doing more listening than speaking. The conversation will probably be awkward at first, but eventually you'll start learning things that you couldn't have discovered in any other way.

January 26

❖ *Release one frustration.*

Inevitably some initiatives don't go as well as we intended. When students try something and don't succeed at it, we call it "education" and urge them to learn from their mistakes. But when something similar happens to us, we regard it as "failure," "disappointment," or even "humiliation." That's a huge semantic difference that can add to our stress and greatly decrease our job satisfaction. While frustration can occasionally be beneficial, causing us to rededicate our efforts and overcome the obstacle, more frequently it's destructive. It prevents us from moving on from a situation that we will never be able to change, try as we might. Wise administrators know when further effort on a project is fruitless and they'd be far better off directing their attention to a much more productive endeavor. Today's suggestion, therefore, is to identify a specific disappointment in your life or career and then let it go. Decide that you've wasted enough time on a situation that for whatever reason hasn't worked out and that you're moving on. Although you may not realize it, people who are close to you probably are already aware that the frustration, disappointment, and regret you've been devoting to this task have been eating away at you (and probably making you less effective at other tasks than you can be). So today, become a student again, and resolve from this point forward to treat your source of frustration as merely part of your learning process.

January 27

❖ *Solve a problem.*

Many goals that academic leaders pursue come to fruition only in the long term. For this reason, you may start thinking that nothing you do matters all that much or that you're not accomplishing anything particularly important. To counteract this feeling, choose one specific problem today, and find a solution. The challenge you take on today needn't be a very big one. In fact, it's probably better if you select a fairly minor, self-contained issue instead of attempting to resolve a significant, highly complex challenge. After all, the goal is to identify a problem, study it, consider various remedies, and solve it—all on the same day. By taking this approach, you'll reinforce for yourself the ways in which you can be most effective in your responsibilities. Of course, not every problem you face will be as easy to solve as the one small challenge you took on today. But use today's success as a metaphor for everything else you achieve in your job. The results may not always be as tangible, but they will certainly be just as genuine.

January 28

❖ *Be distinctive and concise.*

Take a moment to consider a few of the factors that make the discipline, unit, or institution that you serve so distinctive. When you compare it to similar choices available to students, prospective employees, or possible donors, what immediately comes to mind? Refine these ideas until you can describe the distinctive nature of the programs you supervise in twenty-five or fewer words. By doing so, you've created an extremely valuable tool. You'll know exactly what to say when a student asks, "Why should I study here?" or a potential donors asks, "Why should I give you my money when there are so many other important causes?" You can use these thoughts to guide you as you recruit new members of the faculty or staff or when a member of the community inquires about your mission. These short summaries are sometimes called elevator speeches: they provide the essential information in the time that a brief ride on an elevator lasts. Your own elevator speech can help you direct your energy to the things that are really important about your program or institution. Moreover, it can help remind you why what you do is important and improves the lives of others.

January 29

❖ *Set short-term goals.*

We've already dealt several times this academic year with your priorities—both those that fall at the top of your list and those that tend to be far less significant. Today, however, we consider these priorities in a different way. Rather than considering your major long-term objectives, think in terms of your five most important goals for the immediate future. In other words, what are you trying to accomplish this week and this month? How much progress are you making toward reaching these goals? It can be a wonderful long-range goal, for example, to triple the size of your endowment, but it's the more immediate goals, such as touching base with at least one potential donor each day for a week, that'll get you there. So, for today, shorten your perspective from the distant horizon, and focus instead on what's right around the corner. Set five attainable goals that you could accomplish within the next week or two. Then develop a specific plan of action to attain each of them. Place on your calendar tasks related to your goals. Establish clear measures that'll let you know whether you've succeeded. And consider how these five short-term goals help you make progress toward those major priorities that will ultimately be of the greatest benefit to your program.

January 30

❖ *Reach out.*

At even the smallest college, there are bound to be people you don't know as well as you should and perhaps others whom you haven't met at all. At large universities, this problem is compounded many times by the sheer number of faculty members, students, administrators, and members of the staff who are part of the community. Today, go out of your way to introduce yourself to someone at your school you've never met before. Find out where this person is from, what brought him or her to your college or university, and which issues are of most concern to him or her. At the end of the conversation, leave one of your business cards with an invitation to stay in touch.

January 31

❖ *Enjoy a sense of accomplishment.*

Every beginning and every end is an excellent opportunity for reflection. In January, the start of the calendar year encourages us to reflect on our goals for the future and review why we've set those goals. Now, at the end of the month, it's a good time to think about how we've spent the past thirty-one days and gain some satisfaction from what we've achieved. So today look back on everything you've done since the start of the year. If your accomplishments seem substantial, give yourself permission to revel in what you've achieved and to realize that every month can be this productive; all you need to do is manage your time effectively, combine realistic with aspirational goals, and focus your energy on what's truly important. If, however, the past month seems less productive than you hoped it might be, don't waste time regretting lost opportunities. Instead, use today to regain your initiative. Decide right now that you'll be more productive and effective in February. Identify precisely what hindered your work during the past month, and then decide what you can do to overcome these distractions in the future.

February

February 1

❖ *Plan for spontaneity.*

Certain academic administrators seem to be natural planners. They view strategic planning not as a useful tool, but almost as a source of personal joy. They plan continually, mapping out the trajectory for their careers, the long-term growth of their disciplines, even their leisure time. Other administrators appear to be far more spontaneous. They respond, nimbly and with a great deal of entrepreneurial zest, to opportunities as they arise. They immediately see the potential of ideas that others dismiss as eccentric or overly ambitious. If they develop a plan at all, their strategy seems to consist of little more than finding ways to avoid too much planning since they feel constrained by overpreparation. They much prefer having the liberty to take advantage of whatever happens to come their way. If you find yourself identifying with one or the other of these two extremes, today is the day to seek a middle path. If you're a planner, plan for spontaneity. Develop the type of strategy that allows plenty of room for the unexpected, the unpredictable, and the impulsive. Build in time for serendipity, giving yourself permission to follow whatever happens to come along. Develop a plan that allows you to make mistakes, waste some time, and pursue ideas that may turn out to be dead ends. If you're more spontaneous by nature, plan how you might take better advantage of the opportunities that arise unpredictably. Although you don't

169

want to prepare so much that you lose the flexibility you find valuable, try to identify a few ways in which you can be ready to capitalize on the next great idea you encounter.

February 2

❖ *Think metaphorically.*

Like most other professions, academic administration continually attracts new metaphors. It's sometimes said, for instance, that administrators are like institutional fire hydrants: we're capable of putting out a lot of fires, but we also seem to live in a neighborhood that has a lot of dogs. At other times, people may say that administrators are like the pilots of a ship, providing safe guidance through rough waters, but we are the last ones off when everything starts to sink. Today, spend a few minutes identifying the metaphor that you think best describes your job. For instance, are you a detective, always investigating mysteries? Are you a doctor, trying to cure a sick patient "stat"? Are you an explorer, seeking to find a passage into the unknown? Are you a superhero, meek and mild when cloaked in your secret identity but always ready to spring into action the moment a crisis occurs? Use your creativity to develop your own perfect metaphor, and then think about what it reveals about your approach to your work and how you view the challenges of your position.

170

February 3

❖ *Praise sincerely.*

People tend to be quicker to blame than they are to praise. No doubt you receive lots of complaints day after day, but people may rarely notice the good that you do. The sad part of this situation is that many others at your college or university have exactly the same experience. Today's goal is to improve that state of affairs for at least one person. Identify someone who has recently done something excellent—or who is just consistently good every day—and praise that person for his or her contributions. Be as specific as you can in identifying how the person has benefited others. Talk about the impact of this employee's work. Allow the individual sufficient time to bask in the glow of your positive remarks. Compliments like the one you'll give today are all the more meaningful because they arrive unexpectedly. So, don't just settle for one of the usual suspects. Think as broadly as possible about the people who work with you or for you, and choose one whose contributions may have been overlooked. Compliments shouldn't be given with the attitude that "maybe if I praise this person a bit more, he or she will work even harder," but out of genuine recognition for a job well done. After all, your goal today is to make the person's day a little better, not to manipulate an effective employee into contributing even more.

February 4

❖ *Identify a possible successor.*

All academic administrators should have someone in mind who could assume their duties, at least in an acting capacity, if they were suddenly to become unavailable. While all of us may consider ourselves indispensable, none of us really is, and our institutions would manage to get along just fine with someone else in our place. But aside from keeping us humble, there are several other reasons for having a successor in mind. First, it's a good approach to professional development. Identifying a possible successor and grooming that person in the skills needed to do your job will enable the person to grow professionally and may even make that person more successful in his or her current job. Second, it's good emergency planning. In a crisis where you become incapacitated or are needed elsewhere, a possible successor who understands your job can help keep your program going and prevent the emergency from becoming even worse. Third, it can help your own career. It's hard to get promoted or to move on to other responsibilities if you're considered to be indispensable. The best way to help others picture you succeeding in other capacities is to allow them to see someone else doing your current job. Finally, having a possible successor in mind can be liberating. It's hard to go on vacation or devote time to an extended project when no one else can do your job. Delegating routine tasks to a possible successor frees you to do other things, even as it provides important on-the-job training for the person you've chosen.

February 5

❖ *Update your résumé.*

Most academic administrators keep their résumés updated. People ask for a copy of these documents for so many different reasons that it only makes sense to keep them current. But the goal today is to do an even more thorough pruning, purging, expanding, and redesigning your résumé than you usually do. There may be items on it, such as a fairly insignificant local presentation or a long-forgotten task force, that merely add to the document's length without being useful to any possible reader. There may be sections that were ordered in a particular way because it made sense when you were a faculty member but now tend to obscure your role as an administrator. Moreover, many word processing programs come with well-designed templates that can give your résumé a crisper and more professional look. Even if you end up doing little more than tweaking a document with which you're already satisfied, spending some time updating it will have an important benefit: it will help remind you of everything you've done and all the people you've helped along the way. Sometimes reviewing a résumé can be the best possible antidote on a day when you're feeling frustrated or when your efforts don't seem to matter to anyone. It allows you to say, "Look at what I've already accomplished!"

February 6

❖ *Return to the classics.*

There are certain books that every college administrator should read. These are the ones that shaped the way we think about college leadership today, and many of the ideas presented in them remain as pertinent now as they were when the books were originally published. You probably have your own bookshelf of classics. If there is any book in this collection that you had always planned to read but never quite got around to, today's a good day to begin. Or you may decide to reread a work that made a difference in the way you view college administration in order to see whether it still resonates with you as strongly as before. If you're having trouble thinking of which book to read, here are three suggestions, chosen from the many excellent works available:

- Boyer, E. L. (1997). *Scholarship reconsidered: Priorities of the professoriate.* San Francisco: Jossey-Bass. A landmark reassessment of the very nature of what scholarship is and the role it plays in college or university life.

- Seldin, P. (2003). *The teaching portfolio* (3rd ed.). San Francisco: Jossey-Bass. The work that provided higher education with an entirely new way to evaluate effective teaching.
- McKeachie, W. J., & Svinicki, M. (2006). *McKeachie's teaching tips: Strategies, research and theory for college and university teachers* (12th ed.) New York: Houghton Mifflin. *The* book on college-level instruction that every faculty member (and administrator) ought to know by heart.

February 7

❖ *Contact the parent of a student.*

The list of stakeholders at any college or university tends to be long indeed. One practice that many administrators find useful is learning how various issues are perceived by different constituents: students, faculty, staff, alumni, donors and potential donors, community leaders, members of advisory or governing boards—and parents of current students. Today, focus on this last group of stakeholders. Select a parent of a current student and arrange to have an informal chat. Make it clear that you're not calling because the student is in trouble or has done anything wrong. You'd just like to learn a bit more about how today's parents view the institution and the job it's doing in educating their children. Be sure not to reveal any information about the student that may be covered by the Family Educational Rights and Privacy Act of 1974. Most important, don't enter this conversation expecting simply to be praised. There's probably no parent of any current student anywhere who doesn't have at least some concern to raise, suggestion to make, or grievance to air. But those views are being expressed to other people anyway, and certainly it is better for you to be aware of them than to have them discussed behind your back. In many cases, you'll find out about problems you can easily address. In other cases, your sheer willingness to listen will send a strong message to the parent about the type of leadership you're providing. It's likely, too, that you'll find yourself viewing your institution and your own role in it differently as you understand how they're seen through the eyes of others.

February 8

❖ *Immerse yourself in history.*

Nearly every college or university has archives. At relatively new institutions, these files may even extend to the founding of the school. At institutions with longer histories, the documents that are immediately available may stretch back only five or ten years, with earlier records kept in centralized storage. No matter where they are, however, these files can be tremendously informative to read.

Sometimes they reveal that you're still dealing with some of the same challenges that arose decades ago. Sometimes they suggest that the way you do things has changed utterly, and these early records almost appear to be the products of a foreign culture. The advantage of spending some time looking at your school's early history is that it helps you understand the context in which your discipline—or even your institution as a whole—is functioning. Archives can reveal the degree to which decisions were made not in order to achieve some lofty idealistic goal, but out of pure political necessity. They can put you in contact with how your predecessors felt about various important issues and allow you to understand your environment more completely. They can warn you away from policies that repeatedly caused problems before and give you insight into the values of those who helped shape the curriculum. No matter what you discover when you immerse yourself in history, you'll come away with knowledge you could never have gained if you hadn't made a conscious effort to explore the archives.

February 9

❖ *Assess your job satisfaction.*

We often expect that happiness will emerge almost spontaneously from our relationships, our work, and our commitment to certain values. All too rarely, however, do we reflect on whether we're actually obtaining the satisfaction we need from the various parts of our lives and, if not, why not. Today, ask yourself whether your work is making you happy. If it is, what's the cause of this satisfaction? Are you making a difference in people's lives or in the advancement of a discipline? Are you sufficiently but not excessively challenged, working in that zone of proximal development that Lev Vygotsky regarded as most conducive to personal fulfillment? Are the rewards (and think now not just of the *financial* rewards) that you receive from your work proportional to the effort you invest? And if your work is not making you happy, what changes would have to occur to remedy this situation? Does the difficulty seem to be related to the nature of the work itself, the environment in which it occurs, a mismatch between you and the responsibilities you've been assigned, the attitude you bring to your job, or something else? Is it even a problem that can be solved? After all, most administrators are more effective when they're happy in their work. You don't just owe it to yourself; you also owe it to those who depend on you to try to derive as much happiness as you can from the job that you hold.

February 10

❖ *Celebrate someone else's good news.*

Administrators achieve their greatest success not through their own achievements but through creating environments that encourage others to be successful. One effective way of providing that type of encouragement is to reinforce for others how exciting their accomplishments have been. In order to see this principle in operation, identify someone who works with you and has had a major achievement recently. Write that person a note, call or stop by his or her office, and offer warm congratulations on the success that he or she has had. Talk about why that accomplishment is important to students or faculty members and how proud it makes you feel as that person's supervisor. If it seems appropriate to do so, also share the person's good news with others. You'll find that one added benefit of celebrating someone else's good news is that you'll begin feeling better about your own contributions since, through them, you get to work with such talented colleagues.

February 11

❖ *Study your competitors.*

While all our programs and institutions are distinctive in many important ways, it's undeniable that they also share certain features with their peers. In light of this collective experience, choose one of these peers (or rivals) and refresh what you know about it. Visit that institution's Web site and read everything that you have time for. If you have a colleague who works for this school, call him or her and ask about recent developments. What challenges are they facing? What innovations are they developing? Are there any good ideas that you can borrow, keeping in mind that you'll be expected to share a few insights as well? Learning more about our peer institutions—which are often our competitors as well—is one of many ways to stay abreast of current practices in our fields. We can benefit from the experience of others, avoiding the blind alleys that they may have ventured down. Even if you don't learn anything substantive that you may wish to adopt or appropriate, your conversation may cause you to think, "Although we just couldn't do that in our program, what we could do is . . ."

February 12

Offer encouragement.

We often think of administrators as academic leaders because of the direction they provide to the programs they supervise, but they have many other roles to play as well. Administrators can help formulate a vision for the entire college or university, clarify its values, and serve as the voice of the institution to external stakeholders. They can also either improve or reduce the morale of the people who work with them through the tone they take or the remarks they make. Your goal today should thus be to make at least one small change for the better in your area's morale. Identify someone who seems in need of encouragement and offer a few positive remarks. Help the person see the challenges that he or she is facing within a broader context. Offer not blind and superficial optimism, but a realistic assessment of how to improve the situation. You don't want to convey false hope since that actually make matters worse, leaving the impression that you don't understand or care. But a serious conversation that explores the situation from different perspectives and seeks the best possible outcome, rather than the perfect outcome, can help turn a bad situation into one that proves to be manageable for the person. In time, these small steps will lead to a significant improvement in overall morale.

February 13

❖ *Review your evaluation.*

No matter how far any of us rises on the administrative ladder, it's important that we're all evaluated from time to time. While a critical evaluation can be humbling, it's valuable not simply to read these reports once but to take them out periodically throughout the year, read them over, and consider whether any changes have occurred since they were written. If you were commended for certain accomplishments, have you maintained or even increased your strengths in those areas? If you were faulted in any way, what steps have you taken to improve your performance? Even if you strongly disagree with one or more statements in your evaluation, it can be beneficial to reflect on what you have (or have not) done in response to this assessment. Have you made consistent efforts to explain, as clearly and constructively as possible, why you adopted the approaches that you did and established the priorities that you pursued? Have you inadvertently allowed yourself to rest on your laurels when what is really needed is renewed effort and initiative? Occasional review of your latest evaluation helps keep that document from becoming merely a record of the past and allows it to serve as a valuable guide to improvement for the future.

February 14

❖ *Think about potential donors.*

Happy Valentine's Day! Today's a good occasion to spend some time thinking about generosity, gifts, and selfless service. In the world of academic administration, those issues often involve donors to our programs. So, ask yourself, "Who has both the resources to improve the programs I supervise and the interests that might make such a gift a possibility?" If you have a list of potential donors, review that list today. If you've never gathered this information, start doing so. You may well be aware of someone who could provide assistance but to whom you haven't spoken in quite some time. Contact this person, not to ask for a donation, but simply to bring the person up to date on recent developments in your area. Perhaps you can invite the potential donor to an upcoming event and listen to any perspectives this person might share. Programs and institutions rarely receive a transformative gift or even initial contributions because of single calls. Major improvements come about as the result of long histories of close relationships that administrators build. So by reviewing your list of potential donors today, you're taking an important step along the path that can ultimately bring about exciting developments in the programs you lead.

February 15

❖ *Let a faculty member reminisce.*

Last month, you spent some time speaking with a student about his or her favorite professor. Today reverse the process and ask a faculty member to tell you about his or her favorite student. You'll get to know your colleague better from this conversation since the way in which each professor selects his or her most memorable student will tell you a great deal about that professor's values. You'll come away from the exchange seeing the faculty member in a different light, not simply as a member of this or that committee, but as a dedicated professional for whom it's important to build strong ties with students and make a lasting difference in their lives. Particularly if you do not often teach courses yourself, these discussions can be invaluable. They can provide insights into the sorts of students your institution recruits (as opposed to any stereotypes you may have about students today), and you may discover that you have a new sense of pride in the commitment your colleagues have to the students in their courses.

February 16

❖ *Continue your education.*

Today's suggestion involves learning about conferences and meetings that can help you develop the skills you need for your position. New opportunities become available all the time, so there's usually plenty to choose from no matter whether you're a president, provost, vice president, dean, director, or department chair. Good conferences and workshops help us do our jobs with greater vision, efficiency, and creativity. Undoubtedly you're already aware of many of these opportunities. But try today to discover a few that are new to you or that you don't know about as much as you'd like. Start by performing an Internet search on such keywords as "conference," "training," or "workshop" and the title of your position. Then talk to colleagues at other institutions about the meetings and training sessions they attend. Browse through the *Chronicle of Higher Education*'s listing of upcoming events. If at all possible, research at least two or three conferences, workshops, or other training opportunities that you haven't yet taken advantage of but could help you to grow in your position.

February 17

❖ *Track your use of time.*

Take out a note pad or open a word processing file today and, every fifteen minutes or so today, jot down a very brief note about what you've just done. At the end of the day, review how you spent the day by grouping your notes into several categories. Did you spend a lot of the day in meetings? If so, were they meetings that you called and for which you set the agenda, or were you there at the request of others? How much of your day was devoted to appointments? With what types of stake-holders (faculty members, other administrators, students, staff members, external constituents, and so on) did you meet? How much time did you spend answering e-mails, preparing letters, and talking on the phone? How much time did you devote to teaching, scholarship, or community service? After you aggregate your activities into specific blocks of time, examine these categories and see if you can rank them in terms of their importance. Which activities really advanced the mission of your area, and which activities proved not to be the best use of your time? Is there any way in which you can use this insight to become even more effective at the things you regard as most important? Of course, no single day is ever going to be "typical." After all, today may be a day when no classes are in session or when the entire institution is closed for some reason. This type of activity tracking should thus be done periodically throughout the year in order to gain a sense of the general patterns and rhythms of your work.

February 18

❖ *Write yourself a letter of recommendation.*

As an administrator, you probably write letters of recommendation for other people all the time: students need recommendations for jobs or for graduate school; faculty members need these letters to be included in their applications for tenure or promotion, grants, and other opportunities; and sometimes your colleagues or supervisor need letters of reference. Today, however, is all about you. Spend a few minutes writing a letter of recommendation about *yourself*. Your goal should be not necessarily to think about applying for another job (although that's certainly a possibility if it fits into your plans), but rather to get you thinking about how others may regard you. What are likely to appear to an outsider as your greatest strengths and most important contributions? What achievements would one of your references probably emphasize the most? How would the person describe your character? By writing about yourself from the perspective of another person, you'll observe not only your positive qualities but also areas where you may wish to improve.

February 19

❖ *Imagine if money were no object.*

Let's be honest. In higher education, money's *always* an object. There's never enough funding for all the things you need or want to do, and many great ideas never become reality because of a lack of funding. But imagine what might be possible if the situation were different. Complete this sentence, "If money were no object, I would ..." In other words, what would your program or school be like if the sky's the limit? What could you achieve that seems impossible now? How would research improve or students learn better with additional investment? Once you have in mind an image of this exciting possibility, consider whether any aspects of it might be attainable if you could shift your priorities in some way. What could you do less of in order to make at least part of this utopian future a reality? If the dream is compelling enough, there just may be a way to accomplish one or two of its basic elements. But in order to make that dream come true, you first need to have a dream.

February 20

❖ *Offer to be someone's mentor.*

Even if you're just starting out in your administrative position, you've undoubtedly got a great deal of experience that would be invaluable to someone else. By offering to serve as a person's mentor, you'll be providing important service to others. In addition, working as a mentor will cause you to become even more reflective about your own leadership and approaches to various challenges. If you know someone who has already expressed an interest in seeking a higher administrative role, offer to be that person's mentor. Otherwise simply let others know that you're willing to provide this service whenever the need arises. Think of all the things you wish you'd known when you began your first administrative position. Of course, each of us has to experience certain things on our own, but you can help shorten someone else's learning curve and guide others away from mistakes if you express your willingness to act as an administrative mentor.

February 21

❖ *Apologize to someone.*

As much as we hate to admit it, all administrators make mistakes. Sometimes we do the wrong thing because we're acting on the basis of incomplete information, taking a calculated risk that doesn't pan out, or offering advice that turns out to be ill considered. Sometimes our mistakes don't matter very much, but at other times, we cause problems that we seriously regret. We can also make mistakes when we don't listen to people carefully enough, are curt with others, or act without their best interests in mind. Today, identify at least one situation in which you acted in a way that hurt, inconvenienced, or offended someone. Apologize to that person. You may find this suggestion to be one of the most difficult and awkward of all those appearing in this guide. After all, apologies can be uncomfortable to make and uncomfortable to hear. But as a way of improving your overall approach to administration, it's important to make amends to someone for something you now regret, reflect on what you've learned from that situation, and accept that you're going to have to do better in the future.

February 22

❖ *Write a note to a prospective student.*

At most colleges and universities in North America, it's the time of year when applicants are still waiting for admission decisions and haven't yet decided which college or university to attend. In consultation with your institution's admissions office, select a student whom your program or institution is especially eager to recruit, and write a personal note that summarizes a few reasons that your school would be an excellent choice. (This activity thus has a dual benefit: you both reach out to a potential student and strengthen your relationship with the admissions office.) Direct, personal contact will certainly not be possible for every student you hope will join your program, but it can make a real difference in the case of your top two or three choices. Moreover, simply by writing this note, you'll have an opportunity to see the college experience from the student's perspective. What would he or she be most interested in? What would make the opportunities you offer stand out and be truly distinctive? These are the issues to emphasize in what you write.

February 23

❖ *Consider the needs of an employee.*

Spend part of today thinking about how you could assist someone who works for you. Is there any help you can provide that would enable this person to do his or her job better? If you give the matter enough thought, you may see that a particular piece of equipment, software application, or training seminar will be beneficial. Or maybe a redistribution of assignments could free this employee from unproductive tasks to do the sort of work that he or she really does best. It could also be that the person has been hampered in his or her work from being shut out of certain meetings where information crucial to that employee's job is often discussed. The best way to ascertain any person's needs is, of course, simply to ask. But you don't want to do so in a way that implies the person has been ineffective or that what you are proposing is a punishment. You also don't want to give the appearance of promising to do absolutely anything the person might request. After all, the request might be unreasonable or at least beyond your ability to fulfill it. In many cases, however, you'll discover that even a relatively small change can have a remarkable impact on both productivity and morale.

February 24

❖ *Manage your workload.*

One of the challenges that every administrator faces is insufficient time to do everything that's necessary. There are so many problems to solve, so many deadlines to meet, and so many wonderful opportunities to pursue that getting a clear sense of priorities can be difficult. An added challenge is that each administrative position or institution is so different from every other that it's impossible to provide a general rule of thumb saying, "Always do this first and defer that." Remembering that important distinction between the urgent (those duties with the most immediate deadlines) and the important (those opportunities that can make the biggest difference) can be helpful, but ultimately even this distinction doesn't tell administrators what they really need to know. When the time is short and the report is due, that urgent task can begin to seem very important indeed. For this reason, have a conversation today about managing your workload with someone you trust. Find out how that person handles pressure in his or her own position. What strategies does this person use when time is short and the list of obligations is long? The mere fact that you engage in a conversation like this can be helpful. It's useful (not to mention comforting) to know that you're not alone in this situation. It isn't your work ethic that has caused the stress; it's inherent in the position of being an administrator. But aside from gaining the support of someone who knows what you're going through, you'll also probably come away from this conversation with a few suggestions that can assist you in handling your heavy workload.

February 25

❖ *Articulate your vision.*

How would you describe the future that you see for your program or institution? What is it about this vision that excites you? Does the mission of the programs that you supervise expand, or are you simply able to fulfill your current mission better? Spend some time today articulating what you regard as your vision for the future. In addition to envisioning what is possible, pay attention to why that future will be better than what exists now and when these dreams may become reality. Try to enunciate this vision in as compelling and concise a manner as possible. If you write your ideas down, confine your description to a single double-spaced page. If you describe your vision aloud, condense it until you can capture its essence in no more than two or three minutes. If you find your vision powerful enough, begin sharing it with others. What are their reactions? How can you use the vision you've developed today as a guide when you make decisions, set priorities, and allocate resources?

February 26

❖ *Review patterns of expenditure.*

Take a look at your programs' budgets and examine how expenses are tracking relative to the budget of each area that you supervise. You certainly monitor these expenditures on a regular basis anyway, but today's suggestion is to do so in a far more detailed manner. Which areas have expended their budgets at a significantly higher rate than you might expect at this point in the fiscal year? Are there clear reasons for this pattern of spending? For instance, some areas may need to make large purchases of supplies or equipment at the beginning of the academic year and don't need to spend their budgets throughout the entire fiscal period. Other units may have had special circumstances that affected their purchases this year. Your goal today should not be merely to identify all areas where spending patterns are unusual, but also to identify the underlying reasons for these patterns. Since it's only February, there's probably still enough time to make adjustments and correct any problems you discover, but in order to do that, you need to analyze each budget in detail. Similarly, have areas retained surprisingly large unexpended balances? If so, does part of this funding need to be encumbered for purchases that will occur later? Are there areas in which you can balance unanticipated needs with unspent funds from other programs? (Shifting funds is never popular, although it's sometimes necessary.) Devoting time today to studying the budgets that you supervise will help you understand the actual patterns of expense that are occurring in your area and to be proactive in solving identifiable problems before they become too severe.

February 27

❖ *Decide what you would change.*

Just as it can be important for academic leaders to have a positive vision of the future, it can also be valuable for them to have a clear idea of their biggest problems or challenges. Identifying these are your task for today. What's the greatest impediment your school faces that prevents it from achieving its fullest potential? Is there a policy that no longer makes sense, a common perspective that seems unnecessarily narrow, a restriction that continually gets in the way of progress, or a past issue that appears likely to overshadow your future? Don't settle for simplistic answers like, "All our problems could be solved with more money." If limited funding is actually your greatest problem, try to identify realistic reasons that your resources lag behind your current needs, and then explore practical ways of obtaining additional funds. In other words, see if you can determine today where the greatest need for change exists at your institution and what it would take to bring that change about.

February 28

❖ *Read the job listings.*

Job advertisements can be wonderful sources of information. Search committees often place information in these notices about the location and history of the institution, the qualifications of the candidates they are seeking, and the responsibilities of the job itself. It's the last two of these items that can be informative about your current job. Today's suggestion is to look for positions as similar as possible to your job and then determine what you can learn from them. Are there duties that your counterparts frequently are assigned at other institutions that are different from yours? Does the level of staffing appear to be the same for most of these positions? Do other schools seek candidates with experience comparable to what you had when you began your current job, and was that experience useful to you in fulfilling your actual duties? How might the nature of your position have changed since you began? Doing a quick comparison of similar jobs can help you identify additional areas of training you may wish to pursue, changes in staff responsibilities you may wish to initiate, and policies or practices you may wish to adopt. You'll find yourself coming away from this exercise with a better understanding of how you stack up in terms of responsibilities—and perhaps in terms of salary and benefits too—compared to others who hold your current title. Finally, this process may help you clarify the professional direction in which you'd like to develop in the future.

February 29

❖ *Take advantage of a rare gift.*

Today is Leap Year Day, and it's a wonderful opportunity to reflect on rare gifts. Leap Year Day, of course, occurs only every four years, and many of the best opportunities we are given as academic administrators arise only periodically. Today, therefore, see if you can identify one of these rare gifts in your life. Perhaps you'll think of a student you have never forgotten. Or your rare gift could be a mentor who changed your life. *You* might also be the rare gift yourself if you possess a skill or quality that is quite uncommon for someone in your position. No matter what rare gift you identify, consider the importance it has had for you, why you value it, and what that tells you about yourself and your priorities. Then see if you can discover some way to make today's gift of time—a day that each of us experiences only a few dozen times in our lives—particularly meaningful for a current student, a member of the faculty or staff, a colleague, or one of your external constituents.

March

March 1

❖ *Be a philosopher.*

Start this month by reflecting on your own personal
philosophy of administration. If you've never actually
expressed your administrative philosophy before, it may be
helpful to begin by considering exactly why colleges and
universities have department chairs, deans, vice presidents,
provosts, and presidents anyway. What would the
institution be like if these positions didn't exist? What do
academic leaders add to a college or university? How can
schools be helped by good administrators and hampered
by bad ones? Considering these questions will lead you to
home in on how you view your role. For instance, do you
view yourself as the chief arbiter, the person who decides
when an exception to the rules may be permissible? Or
are you more of a catalyst, inducing change and activity all
around you while remaining relatively unaffected yourself?
Do you see yourself as a coach, setting the bar as high
as possible and motivating others to achieve goals they
once thought impossible? Are you a repairman, fixing one
problem after another as you encounter them? Are you a
visionary, always looking into the future and considering
what might be? Undoubtedly you will conclude that you
must assume each of these roles from time to time. But
which of them tends to be your default position? Why
do you do the things that you do in the way that you do

them, and, on a fundamental level, what are you trying to accomplish?

March 2

❖ *Think of something outrageous.*

Challenge yourself today to imagine the most outrageous, outlandish idea you can think of related to programs that you supervise. The goal of this exercise is not to concentrate on anything even remotely possible or attainable, but to free your imagination so that it runs as wild as it can. The reason for engaging in this exercise is to stoke your creativity. Sometimes we become so bogged down in administrivia that we can hardly see beyond the next budget proposal, program review, or personnel action form. But allowing yourself to think occasionally of something that is absolutely impossible by its very nature can help you become more innovative when you next need to stretch the limits of what is actually possible. What could your program be like if every faculty position were endowed or every major was on full scholarship? What might it mean if each of your undergraduate students could study abroad for a full year at no cost to them, and each of your graduate students could present his or her research at a major international conference? How might morale be improved if each faculty member received a full year's sabbatical every three years? With models like these in mind, ask yourself what sort of ridiculous ideas you can generate and what it is about them that makes them so ridiculous anyway. What assumptions do you find yourself making about your school and its future that distinguish what's realistic from what's ludicrous? And what might happen if you were to start questioning those assumptions?

March 3

❊ *Reread your institution's strategic plan.*

As you are with your institution's mission statement, you are probably already quite familiar with your school's strategic plan. You may even have played a part in writing it. Even so, it is worthwhile every now and then to read over the entire plan and look at it with new eyes. In this way, you'll keep these long-term objectives fresh in your mind while you make day-to-day decisions. As you read the strategic plan from start to finish, look for areas in which you are making good progress toward attaining the goals outlined there. Identify as well areas where you have not been quite as successful. Consider whether some situations have changed in ways that couldn't have been predicted when the strategic plan was being developed. Most important, see if you can identify something that you could do today in order to advance the objectives outlined in the plan.

March 4

❖ *Invite a member of the staff to lunch.*

Colleges and universities couldn't function without a dedicated staff to support them. Often these employees are inadequately paid, receive very little respect in an institution where advanced degrees and faculty status are valued more than anything else, and yet perform tasks each day that are absolutely essential to the school's success. Invite one of these staff members to lunch today. Express your gratitude for what the person does. In fact, find out everything that the person does. (You may well be surprised at how much the employee's duties entail.) Discover the issues that are most important to this person. For example, what are the most satisfying parts of his or her job? What are the biggest frustrations? How would the staff member describe his or her most important contribution to the work of the institution? This conversation will give you a much greater appreciation for the many roles that most staff members play in higher education, and you'll have made at least one of them feel more appreciated by your efforts.

March 5

❖ *Describe a "typical" student.*

"What are your students like?" is a fairly common question for people to ask if they don't know your institution or program very well. How do you answer that question when it is posed? And how might your answer cause the listener to draw conclusions about your college or university? Certainly there is no such thing as a typical student. Every student has unique needs, goals, and characteristics. But we frequently know, when speaking to a prospective student, whether he or she is likely to fit in or succeed in our programs. What are the impressions that lead you to make these judgments? Do most of the students you meet on campus march to the beat of their own drummer, or are they a bit more traditional? Do they all want to save the world, or do they tend to be motivated by dreams of personal success? Do they come to you already bright and accomplished, or do you see your school's mission as helping to develop students who have not yet had a chance to reach their potential? No school will suit every type of student, and no student will be happy in every type of school. Knowing the profile of the students who are attracted to, succeed at, and graduate from your institution can help you in innumerable ways. It can assist you in tailoring your message when recruiting students for your program. It can help you build a case statement for a potential donor. It can lead you to refocus the proposal for a grant. It can even help you recommit to the importance of the tasks you perform every day.

March 6

❖ *Take a personality test.*

Knowing your long-term goals as an academic administrator frequently emerges from knowing precisely who you are right now. For this reason, spend some time today taking one of the standard personality inventories, even if you've already taken them many times. The test you take is relatively unimportant for today's purposes. Common inventories of this type are the Myers-Briggs Type Indicator, the Keirsey Temperament Sorter, and the DISC Personality Profile. If there's one of these that you haven't yet taken, you might start with that, just to see if its results are different from the others. Find out what the test reveals about your personality and your approach to interacting with others. Do you believe that you've changed significantly over time? If you had taken this test every ten years throughout your life, would the results have been consistent, or would there have been significant differences in certain periods? Don't let the results of the test become too prescriptive for you. They should help you understand a few things about who you are, not dictate who you must become. But if you do learn something about yourself that hadn't occurred to you before, think of ways in which this new information can help you become more successful in your professional relationships. Begin with congratulating yourself now in understanding a few additional things about who you are. Your next exciting opportunity, then, will be to continue discovering all that you're capable of becoming.

March 7

❖ *Analyze trends.*

Issues come and go in the history of higher education. Some of these turn out to be nothing more than fads; they may seem highly important for a short time but quickly pass into irrelevance. Other issues transform the very enterprise of higher education, and administrators ignore them at their peril. If you consider all the issues that are discussed in higher education today, which do you regard as the most important? Have these issues affected the way you do your job? If so, how? If not, why not? As you look to the future, which of the concerns that administrators have today seem likely to be regarded someday as of only temporary concern? Which are most likely to have an impact for some years to come? Consider ways in which you can help position your unit or institution so as to take full advantage of the trends that are likely to be important in the years ahead.

March 8

❖ *Be your own consultant.*

Each program at a college or university can benefit by having an outside consultant come in from time to time to examine current policies and procedures and make recommendations about needed changes. External reviewers can provide a frank and candid objectivity, and although they may misunderstand certain features of your program because they don't know it intimately, they often see issues in a different light from those who work in that environment day after day. Consultants can help you understand how your programs look to external constituents and see the elephant in the room that everyone around you knows is there but no one wishes to talk about. While you can't receive all the benefits of this type of review by doing it yourself, it can be a useful exercise to say, "If I were a consultant brought here by my own institution, and if I were both candid and objective, what would I say our greatest strengths were? What would I identify as our greatest weaknesses? What recommendations would I make about how to proceed for the future?" Your "consultant's report" need not be long— a single page or two will be sufficient—but it can be revealing to assess your own program applying the same standards you would adopt when reviewing a program at a peer institution. Don't leave yourself out of the evaluation: consider ways in which you contribute to your program's success, as well as ways in which you could do better in the future.

March 9

❖ *Envision your dream job*.

If you could have the perfect job at the perfect college or university in the perfect location, what would you be doing? Develop the clearest possible image of what you would regard as your dream job, and then identify all the aspects of it that make that image so enticing for you. Would you be doing only the work you enjoy and feel successful at doing if you were to have this job? Would all of your colleagues be responsible and supportive? Would the values of the institution more closely reflect your own? Would the facilities be better and the institution more fully equipped to fulfill the mission that you regard as important? Try to clarify for yourself precisely what it is that you are changing from your current situation as you create this mental image. Are the improvements you imagine mostly in the people around you, your physical environment, your job responsibilities, your remuneration package, or something else? When you identify precisely what makes your dream job so wonderful, you may sometimes discover that you are capable of instituting at least some of those changes right now in your current position. In other words, take that mental image of your perfect work environment and use it as a blueprint to move your current job as close as possible toward that new reality. You may well discover that even one or two small changes can improve immeasurably how effective you are in your position and how much you enjoy what you do.

March 10

❖ Explore your faculty's scholarship.

One of the keys to good administration is catching the people with whom you work doing something right. And the better you understand their approaches to teaching, research, and service, the easier it will be to see their strengths in a variety of areas. Today, continue this process by reading an article by one of your faculty members or by starting to read one of his or her books. The work of scholarship that you select need not be in a field closely related to your own; it may even be better for your own professional development if you immerse yourself in work that's relatively remote from your discipline. If you hold an administrative position in which you do not directly supervise faculty members or where the faculty members who report to you are not expected to engage in scholarly publication, then familiarize yourself with whatever accomplishments you would regard as most comparable to refereed research. What you will learn will help you in your efforts to recruit students, solicit donor support, evaluate faculty members, and perform a variety of other administrative tasks. It will also help you understand a bit better the research philosophy of at least one of your faculty members, creating a bridge for you that may not have otherwise existed.

March 11

✳ *Reallocate 5 percent of your budget.*

If you want to gain the clearest and most objective sense of what your real priorities are, examine your budget. In other words, it can be easy to say, "Achieving this goal is the single most important thing we do," but if your allocation of resources belies that claim, you're engaging in hollow rhetoric. In order to test how closely your area's budget actually reflects your greatest priorities, perform a mental experiment today. Imagine that you were under a mandate to reallocate 5 percent of your continuing budget. For the purposes of this exercise, don't allow yourself to say anything like, "But I can't do that. I don't have any expenditures that aren't absolutely vital to our mission." Force yourself to target the lowest-priority 5 percent of your budget, no matter how difficult that may be to identify, and envision how you would reallocate that funding to personnel and other continuing expense categories. Performing this thought experiment each academic year serves two useful purposes. First, it helps you prepare for those times—and don't deceive yourself: they will come—when you are forced to prepare quickly for an unanticipated midyear budget reduction. Second, it may alert you to ways in which you're able to make progress toward achieving higher priorities by shifting funding from lower ones. There are times, you'll discover, when this mental exercise can provide the prelude to an actual and beneficial reallocation.

March 12

❖ *Identify your most wasteful practice.*

The various activities that occur at a college or university can be wasteful in several ways. Some of our practices waste time. Others waste money or other scarce resources. Still others might waste an opportunity to do something of more lasting importance. Take one small step today to improve efficiency and sustainability. Review your own administrative practices, and see if you can identify one of them that is particularly wasteful or inefficient. For instance, suppose you regularly have meetings that require participants to travel from great distances. Think about whether it might be possible to reduce the frequency of these meetings, conduct them by telephone or videoconference, or phase them out entirely. With the time, energy, or resources that you save, what might you be able to achieve that would be far more meaningful to your long-term goals? If you're creative enough in identifying these inefficient uses of resources, you may even discover a way to fund that 5 percent of your budget that you were seeking to reinvest yesterday.

March 13

❖ *Think big.* Really *big.*

Large financial gifts are extremely rare in academia.
Large unrestricted gifts are even rarer. But suppose
that one came your way. Conduct a thought experiment
today. Complete the following sentence: "If my program
[institution] suddenly received an unrestricted grant of
$100 million, I would use it to . . ." What would you be
able to achieve under such a scenario that's impossible
now? How could your entire program or institution be
transformed, and why would that transformation matter?
Conducting this type of mental exercise is important
because it lends more precision to your vision for the
future. After all, a strategic plan is important, but an
institution's budget is the real plan. So this imaginary
budgeting encourages you to flesh out your most
innovative ideas. Besides, this thought experiment will
give you an answer that you can use (or at least adapt)
the next time a potential donor asks, "Why should I
make a contribution to your area? What difference
would it make?" You may never be in a position to
see every detail of your most ambitious vision become
a reality, but developing this vision will be extremely
useful to you whenever any opportunity to shape the
future arises.

March 14

❖ *Develop five new interview questions.*

Almost all administrators interview candidates for jobs from time to time. Perhaps this is even the most important aspect of your job. Regardless of how often you interview candidates, there's a problem with any activity we do repeatedly: our approach to it can become stale over time. Most interviewers revert to the same questions in every interview. Although the issues those questions address may be comfortable and familiar, they may not reveal everything we need to know. So today, set yourself the task of developing five new questions to ask candidates who are interviewing for a job. You can invent the questions yourself, scout Web pages on such topics as "effective interview questions," get a few ideas from your colleagues, or browse through books that deal with interview techniques. The source of the questions is far less important than their ability to provide you with new insights. If we ask the same questions over and over, we gradually start thinking of certain answers as being "right" and all others as "wrong." We unconsciously compare one candidate's answers to another even if they're not in the same search and even if their interviews occurred years apart. New questions will keep you fresh during interviews. Because you don't know the answers that candidates frequently give, you'll find yourself listening to the answers more attentively and thus gaining insights you may not have had otherwise.

214

March 15

❖ *Challenge your own leadership style.*

Today brings us to the Ides of March, the day when Julius Caesar was assassinated and the Roman Republic began a long and bloody civil war. It's thus a good time for leaders at all levels to reflect on just how effective their administrative style has been. Remember that a leader isn't a really leader if no one is following and that not all the daggers that threaten us are literal ones. The Ides of March is a good day to reflect on the extent to which we're connecting with and properly motivating the people who report to us. It's perfectly fine, even highly appropriate, for leaders to take a firm stand on issues that are truly significant or matter deeply to them. But not every issue is one that you'll be willing to fight to the death over. Have you demonstrated flexibility and responsiveness wherever you can and resolution and commitment wherever it's necessary? Have you found the appropriate balance between being a dictator and trying to be everyone's friend? Have you avoided factionalism, conveying fairness and openness to opposing points of view? Do you ever separate yourself from your employees, distinguishing between "us" and "them" and speaking disparagingly of faculty, staff, or students? What has been particularly effective about your leadership style, and what aspects of your approach could use some adjustment? Conduct this type of self-inventory today, and see if there are ways in which you can advance your program's most important goals without "getting assassinated" in the process.

March 16

❖ *Recall a poor judgment.*

Even the most perceptive people sometimes misjudge others. Perhaps someone's appearance misled us or our first acquaintance with someone got off on the wrong foot. Think back to one of these incidents today. If you've been guilty of a poor judgment that still affects your relationship with that person, today is the perfect time to put all of that behind you and move forward in a more productive manner. If the situation has already been resolved, consider instead any lessons that you may have learned from your misjudgment. How can you prevent yourself from making this kind of mistake in the future? Does it give you any insights you can share with others who are developing their own administrative skills?

March 17

❖ *Relax. You've earned it.*

College administration can be stressful. We encounter budget crises, personnel conflicts, pending deadlines, unreasonable demands, and unbelievable amounts of paperwork. But if you focus only on these challenges, you'll find yourself becoming less and less effective, perhaps even experiencing a sense of burnout over time. One of the ways to prevent this problem is to build periodic opportunities for relaxation into your schedule. Start this practice today, and give yourself permission to enjoy ten minutes of complete relaxation without checking e-mail, answering the telephone, receiving visitors, or doing anything that is even remotely work related. How you choose to relax is up to you. You might prefer to enjoy silence in a darkened room. You can listen to your favorite kind of music. You can take a short nap or a brief stroll. The basic idea is that what you do is far less important than the commitment to do something. Today's ten-minute period of relaxation is not a waste of time but an investment in good administration. After it's completed, you'll return to your tasks renewed and with a greater sense of energy or commitment.

March 18

❖ *Identify a pressure point.*

What aspect of your work tends to cause you the most aggravation? Is it when you discuss a particular issue—maybe some topic where your views are dramatically different from those of your colleagues? Or do you find it especially frustrating to deal with a particular group of stakeholders, such as faculty members in a certain discipline or the press, who oppose the general direction in which you're leading your programs? Do you become aggravated in certain environments, such as during promotion reviews or budget hearings? Today's suggestion is to identify the source of your greatest resistance and then to consider what it means. You may discover that even though it's annoying, this opposition is healthy—a force that prevents you from taking action without considering all alternatives. Constructive opposition can save a college or university from groupthink on important issues. Or you may decide that the amount of opposition you're receiving is largely destructive and that better ways must be found to unite all constituents in order to address the institution's needs. You may even learn that the friction you are experiencing results from poor communication and that the irritation dissipates when better information is shared. In other words, identify your greatest source of opposition, but understand that not all opposition is bad. Sometimes what we need to change most is not the conflict itself but our attitudes about the conflict. Even when discord is truly destructive to an institution, we need first to identify its ultimate source before we can develop an effective plan to alleviate it.

March 19

❖ *Remember good administrative advice.*

At some point in your administrative career, someone must have given you a piece of advice that has been particularly important to you over the years. Perhaps you had a trusted mentor or a colleague you admired for his or her keen insight. The advice that person shared with you may have been completely original or it may have been a much-repeated truism like, "No good deed goes unpunished" or, "College administration is like herding cats." Regardless of the source and nature of the best advice you ever received, reflect on it today and see if you can recall several occasions when you profited from this bit of wisdom. Is there someone you work with now who could benefit from a similar word of advice from you?

March 20

❖ *Make your environment more accessible.*

We don't always see things when we encounter them day after day. For this reason, assemble a few students today and ask them for suggestions about ways in which your workspace could be improved. What would it take to make your desk, office, or entire department feel more open and accessible? If you're a university president, the area you discuss might be your entire campus, or perhaps several campuses. If you're a department chair, your conversation might extend to the classrooms, labs, and studios commonly used by your discipline. Undoubtedly your conversation will be of an entirely different nature if you work for a program that primarily serves graduate or postdoctoral students than what administrators might learn if they work in an exclusively undergraduate program. But whatever your individual situation, the primary goal of the conversation should be the same: What could you do to make the space in which you work more welcoming, to make students feel that they belong here? Some of the suggestions will be wholly impractical, while others could be implemented at little or no cost. In any case, you'll learn something valuable about how others see your physical workspace. You may discover that you've been sending messages about your priorities and values that you never intended.

March 21

❖ *Review your computer files.*

It's easy to think of the files on your computer as your own private property. In reality, however, your work computer is far more public than you may realize. If you live in a state with an open records law, it may be relatively easy for someone to file an information request and gain access to documents that you regard as highly confidential. Moreover, if your computer is networked, as almost all work computers are now, it is possible for other people to view every file on your computer, even to see your screen precisely in the way that it looks to you. There are many reasons, therefore, for taking stock of what's on your computer, purging it of materials that violate your institution's appropriate use policy or that could prove damaging if made public. You should never write anything in an e-mail that you would not want quoted in the local paper. That's actually a good rule to apply to every document on your computer. Be sure you don't retain music or video files that were illegally downloaded, since these could compromise your institution's ability to have access to information. Eliminate any images, documents, or sound files that would be difficult or embarrassing to justify if others knew that you had them. In general, treat your entire hard drive as though it were always available to people who don't know you and don't have your best interests in mind. Delete, too, out-of-date personnel materials unless you are required by law or institutional policy to retain them. At best, these files take up room that's better devoted to other purposes. At worst, they may contain confidential information, such as Social Security numbers, that can lead to identity theft or other forms of misuse.

March 22

❖ *Learn something new about strategic planning.*

There's so much that we all need to learn about strategic planning that, no matter whether it's critical to your job or only a topic that you hear about from time to time, it's beneficial to find out more about this subject. Strategic planning is firmly established as a key process by which institutions of higher education prepare for the future (and, quite frankly, some schools do it better than others). In a properly designed strategic planning process, a seamless flow of procedures should extend from review of the school's fundamental mission through the establishment of long-term goals (*strategic visioning*) to the development of implementation plans at each level of the institution (*strategic implementation*) to continual assessment of results, and back again to explore how those results echo and possibly shape the mission of the institution. Certainly, a complex, multicampus, comprehensive university will do a very different kind of strategic planning from what may occur at a liberal arts college, conservatory, or seminary. However, new approaches and best practices for all types of institutions are regularly presented in journals and at conferences. For this reason, spend a few minutes today learning at least one substantive thing about strategic planning that you don't yet know. You'll probably discover that anything you learn will have an application in your day-to-day responsibilities sooner than you can imagine.

March 23

❖ *Identify a bad habit.*

Some things we do intentionally: we're fully conscious of both the reasons for our actions and their probable results. But other things we do simply by habit. Perhaps we've fallen into a routine, repeating the things we've done before simply because they are familiar. Not all of these habits are bad habits, of course. A person who has a habit of greeting everyone he or she meets on campus may help convey the sense that the community is a welcoming and friendly place to be. But other habits waste precious resources and divert energy from more productive activities. Reflect on various things that you do—and why you do them—as you go about your work today. If you have a trusted mentor or confidant, ask that person whether he or she has noticed any bad habits you may have. A deeply ingrained habit can be very hard to break, but doing so can free up time and energy that you may not be spending as effectively as you could and can ultimately help you be successful in whatever position you hold.

March 24

❖ *Empower others.*

Delegation means assigning responsibility to others. Empowerment entails assigning authority to others. As we saw back on December 18, too often in higher education, responsibility and authority don't go hand in hand. For example, an assistant dean or office administrator may have a tremendous amount of responsibility, but almost no authority to ensure that others complete their assignments in an efficient and successful manner. Today, take one small step in reversing this trend. Give someone who works for you the full ability he or she needs in order to carry out an important task. Make it clear to everyone else in your unit that when this person speaks, he or she does so on your authority. Specify that your designee's decisions carry the full weight of your position and that, within the limits of the duties that you've assigned, this person is completely in charge. If this experiment doesn't prove to be successful, see if you can determine whether it is the person you've selected, your own management style, your institution, or the task itself that has made the desired outcome so difficult. But if the experiment does succeed, consider whether you can build on this success, empowering others in such a way that benefits your institution even as it decreases your workload.

March 25

❖ *Find a hot-button issue.*

Every campus or program has at least one issue that people care deeply about. This is the issue that comes up repeatedly in hallway conversations, derails the agenda at meetings of the faculty or staff, and becomes the subject of numerous heated e-mails. People are so emotionally involved in this particular issue that they often get angry when they talk about it. Opinions about what should be done tend to run deep, although there is rarely widespread agreement about the best course of action to take. Today, try to identify what issue on your campus best fits this description. What impact might the outcome of this issue have on the future success of your programs? Are there ways in which you can channel the passion people feel about this issue into a constructive plan of action? What might your role be as a leader in a matter that is obviously of great concern to those who work with you?

March 26

❖ *Increase opportunities for research.*

Earlier this month, you were given an opportunity to become more familiar with the scholarship of a faculty member at your college or university by reading one of that professor's articles or books. Today, carry that effort even further by making a specific effort to address the scholarship, research, or creative activity at your entire institution. The type of initiative you undertake today will depend on the focus and mission of your school. You may be working at a major research university where large grants and government contracts are vital to what you do. Or you may be working at a community college where priority is given to teaching and service, with research occurring primarily in certain undergraduate projects, institutional self-studies, and the efforts of individual faculty members. Or your situation may fall somewhere between. The point is that in higher education, research is important to what everyone does, whether it relates to making major new discoveries, helping students pursue innovative ideas, or figuring out how to improve your own policies and procedures. Spend some time today considering the impediments that are preventing the programs you supervise from achieving their full potential in the area of research. What are your long-term goals in the area of scholarship, research, or creative activity? Make it your goal today not to solve all problems you face in this area, but to develop a single practical idea for advancing your overall research agenda. It may well take weeks, months, or even years for your goal to be achieved, but today you will have established a clear, viable direction in which to proceed.

March 27

❖ *Reflect on your proudest accomplishment.*

Sometimes we get so caught up in solving problems and dealing with conflicts that we forget all the important things we've already accomplished. Today, take a few minutes and think of your proudest accomplishment as an academic administrator. What have you done that helped improve someone's life, made a program more effective, opened up a new source of funding, or resolved a troubling issue? Does the specific achievement that first occurred to you when you began this exercise reveal something about your priorities and values? Your memories today should give you a sense of pride and satisfaction, and you'll want to tap back into those feelings whenever you have to deal with an issue that's particularly frustrating or appears insoluble. Are there any challenges or opportunities you face right now that are similar to your proudest achievement? If so, use your experience and demonstrated record of success to guide you in your next major accomplishment.

March 28

❖ *Improve your public presentations.*

Academic administrators frequently have to speak in public. You may need to speak to groups of prospective students whom you're trying to recruit to your program, address members of the faculty and staff in regular meetings, interact with committees of your peers, report to legislators or trustees, or make occasional presentations to all kinds of groups, both large and small. No matter how effective you already are in making public presentations, everyone can improve their skills through practice, critique, and training. Today, look for chances to get even better in this area. You might explore the possibility of formal training at an administrative workshop or short course. Or you might simply prefer to gain as much practice as possible by volunteering to speak in front of as many groups as you can. Regardless of the plan you pursue, you'll inevitably become more comfortable and effective at one of the tasks that every administrator finds essential.

March 29

❖ *Examine your use of pronouns.*

The way in which someone uses personal pronouns can be revealing. For instance, people who mention a hypothetical faculty member and use only the pronoun *he* convey the message that they don't immediately think of women as college professors. Similarly, an administrator whose remarks are filled with *I*, *me*, and *my* seems to be focused only on his or her achievements, not those of everyone else who contributes to the program. Some administrators like to adopt such phrases as *my faculty* and *my students*, believing that these expressions demonstrate a strong personal interest in the success of others. But those same phrases can strike some people as possessive or paternalistic, suggesting that speaker regards even the accomplishments of others as resulting from his or her own leadership. Many academic leaders find that the pronouns *we*, *us*, and *our* are far more inclusive and convey a sense of shared purpose and commitment. With this observation in mind, pay close attention to your own speech patterns today, considering in particular whether the personal pronouns you use convey any unintended and undesirable subliminal messages to others.

March 30

❖ *Explore a few other best practices in higher education.*

Choose some specific aspect of your current job and investigate how it's done at other colleges or universities. The topic you choose to investigate shouldn't be too large since you don't want to undertake a task that will overwhelm your day. For instance, if you work in admissions, don't select a topic as broad as the entire issue of student recruitment. Rather, focus on something more specific, like cultivating relationships with high school counselors, how recruitment strategies can be targeted toward certain disciplines or geographical areas, integrating the admissions office with financial aid programs, and the like. In a similar way, if you are an administrator of an academic area, don't try to identify best practices relating to everything you do. Choose instead a topic of particular concern to you, such as general education reform, encouraging under-graduate research, or building cooperative programs with local industries. Then conduct an Internet search on such terms as "best practices student remediation college alge-bra" or others related to the topic you chose. This exercise shouldn't take you very long, but don't stop until you get at least one idea that's worth discussing with your colleagues. You may discover that even ideas that aren't appropriate for your institution or program can be adapted or modified in a way that makes them useful. Get your colleagues dis-cussing the example of best practices that you've discovered and find out whether they've recently encountered any best practices of their own.

March 31

❖ *Finish something.*

Bring March to a close in a way that leaves you with a sense of accomplishment. Go through the various projects and activities that you've begun throughout the year, and complete at least one of them. Don't choose something that you would need to finish hastily or in an unsatisfactory manner. Rather, select some project that is near fruition anyway or has continued long enough as it is. Sometimes we extend projects and reports long past the point where we are still making useful improvements. Even if the task you complete today is relatively minor, the sense of achievement you feel when it's done is likely to be significant. In addition, concluding an activity often provides an antidote we need whenever we start feeling that nothing can be completed in higher education until we study absolutely every alternative and consider all possible options. You're not going to get caught in that trap today. You're going to end the month with an ongoing project from your to-do list checked off as complete.

April

April 1

❖ *Do something foolish.*

Today is April Fools' Day, the day traditionally dedicated to practical jokes and public humiliations. In keeping with the spirit of the day, resolve to do something foolish, like wearing that flashy tie or scarf if you usually dress conservatively. The idea of this exercise isn't to try something that would embarrass you, harm your program, or undermine your authority. Rather, the goal today is to grant yourself permission to do one thing today that departs from the norm, breaks a self-imposed rule, seems a little daring, or challenges a preconceived notion. Do something that people wouldn't ordinarily expect you to do. Surprise those who know you and, even more important, surprise yourself with what you're capable of.

April 2

❖ *Audit your committees and meetings.*

If you're like most other administrators, you probably spend a significant part of each day in meetings. Today, perform an audit of all the committees on which you serve and all the meetings you regularly attend. Rank them from the most important and productive down to the least essential and worthwhile. Do any groups on your list meet more frequently than they need to and end up wasting their members' time? If so, how can you go about improving this situation? Is reducing the frequency of these meetings within your own authority, or would you need to confer with someone else? Have any groups on your list outlived their usefulness? Do important decisions end up being made in ways that lead to problems because the wrong people were involved in the discussions? Can some of these groups be consolidated or streamlined so as to make more efficient use of everyone's time? Do some of the groups meet just for routine updates and to exchange information when other forms of communication would be more effective? As you conduct this audit, use as a central criterion the goal of determining how the programs you supervise can reach the best decisions in the most timely manner by involving the right people. If changes need to occur that are outside your own sphere of authority, work collegially with those who are responsible for this area to bring about an improvement that will be useful to all concerned.

April 3

❖ *Reread your institution's disaster plan.*

The worst time to start getting acquainted with your institution's disaster plan is during a disaster. By the time a crisis occurs, you'll be far too busy handling important details and making quick decisions to be investigating what your institution's policies are and how you should be responding. Besides, many disaster plans contain extremely helpful advice that can prevent catastrophic situations from developing in the first place. So take a few minutes today to reacquaint yourself with your school's disaster plan. Be sure you know which people you're expected to contact in an emergency and what your first actions should be in these situations. Update your calendar with a note to review the disaster plan again in a year so that you'll always be aware of changes and have the information it contains fresh in your mind.

April 4

❖ *Reward yourself.*

You've worked hard this academic year, and there have probably been a number of unanticipated frustrations and problems that you've experienced along the way. It's time to reward yourself for all of the hard work you've invested in your job this year. The reward need not be something expensive. You could take some extra time to enjoy an activity you particularly like. Go to a movie. Spend an hour at an art gallery. Take a stroll through the park. Or buy yourself a present. College administrators make so many contributions that go unnoticed by others that you could wait a very long time before either your supervisor or your employees acknowledge your achievements. For today, notice your accomplishments yourself, and take pride in the efforts you have made.

April 5

❖ *Define your purpose.*

In order to remain effective, academic administrators need to reflect periodically on the nature of their own leadership. In other words, it's important to have a clear sense not only of what you're trying to accomplish, but also why you lead in the way that you do. For instance, if you view yourself largely as a change agent, what is it about change (either universally or in your specific situation) that makes it seem so desirable? If you're trying to expand one of the programs you supervise, what better purpose will it be able to serve if it's larger? If you see your role as that of consensus builder, what do you hope to achieve through broad-based agreement that couldn't be achieved better through creative and constructive conflict? Asking these questions is important because they prevent us from assuming that there's only one approach to take. Every now and then, we need to challenge ourselves in terms of how we define our roles as academic leaders and ask why each role that we've adopted is the best for ourselves or for our institution. So today, make a conscious effort to define the purpose of your leadership in order to make it easier for you to achieve that purpose successfully.

April 6

❖ *Assess faculty and staff morale.*

One of the truisms of higher education is always that "morale today is lower than it's ever been." While that observation may seem a bit cynical, it reflects the tendency many people have to idealize their past sense of community and job satisfaction. The truth is that there have always been challenges to faculty and staff morale and that many people find that their initial enthusiasm for their jobs wanes over time. So, setting aside this common feeling that morale *must* be declining, see if you can gauge how members of the faculty and staff feel about the community in which they work. What are the issues that are causing people to become disengaged from the institution or to feel that their efforts have gone unappreciated? In which areas does commitment seem higher or people seem to be happier in their jobs? Can you think of any specific actions you could take to alleviate certain causes of low morale or enhance those environments where morale seems good? Many administrators think of faculty and staff morale as a mere by-product of what they do, but one of the quickest ways to destroy it is to fail repeatedly to address it. Avoid this mistake today by doing at least one substantive thing to improve morale.

April 7

❖ *Sort through a stack of papers.*

Most academic leaders find that documents arrive in their offices much faster than they can be processed effectively. Certain papers aren't important enough to file permanently but are still too important to throw away immediately. They thus they land on our desks and remain there long after they're no longer needed. So, if you've fallen behind in handling the paperwork that has come your way, set yourself the goal of sorting a single stack of papers today. Keep your expectations manageable. If you resolve to go through everything that has accumulated since the start of the academic year, you're likely to find the task so overwhelming that you'll end up accomplishing very little. It's far better to concern yourself with a single stack of papers and deal with it completely. For each item, decide whether to throw it away, forward it to someone else, file it, or act on it immediately yourself. When you've finished this task, you may discover that you have such a sense of relief that you'll want to continue this process once every week or two. Consider adopting a regular, but not overly ambitious, sorting schedule, and you'll greatly reduce the number of stacks that are turning into mulch in your office while increasing your efficiency in the process.

April 8

❖ *Expand your knowledge of higher education law.*

One aspect of higher education that every administrator needs to learn more about is the law as it applies to
colleges and universities. Higher education law is constantly changing, and it affects the way in which every
academic leader makes decisions and the manner in which
they interact with all of their stakeholders. Conferences
and workshops on higher education law take place at many
locations throughout the academic year, so there will be
at least one not far way from you that you can attend. If
even short-distance travel is an issue, there are periodic
online workshops on higher education law that you can
participate in from your desk. A good training session
on higher education law should summarize for you how
recent developments in case law affect you, your faculty,
and your students. It should also leave you feeling just ner-
vous enough about potential legal problems that you give
careful consideration to the policies and procedures under
your control. Each administrator should make an effort to
refresh his or her knowledge about the law at least once a
year in order to stay abreast of recent developments and
to ask questions that may have arisen in his or her professional area.

April 9

❧ *Build a bridge.*

Higher education thrives on partnerships. Research teams, interdisciplinary courses, cooperative programs, and consortia all involve building bridges between people, programs, or institutions. Today, consider ways in which the area that you supervise can cooperate effectively with one of its peers or competitors in order to achieve a greater good. If you're the chair of a department or the dean of a college, look for opportunities to unite your efforts with another program, at your own school or a similar institution in order to create innovative opportunities for students. If you're a vice president, how can you partner with other vice presidential divisions in order to achieve something distinctive or more cost-effective? If you're a president, chancellor, or rector, explore ways of cooperating with one of your peer institutions so that the research efforts or quality of education will be improved at both schools. These types of partnerships are particularly pleasing to external stakeholders, such as donors and members of the advisory or governing board, because they allow the institution to break out of traditional academic silos and make more innovative use of existing resources.

April 10

❖ *Learn a new software application.*

Technology changes rapidly. Since the last time you looked (even if it was yesterday), new equipment and software applications have become available that can be useful in your teaching and research environments. Although it's impossible to keep up with every new development in information technology, most administrators can do a better job learning about the improvements that matter most to their faculty and students. Set yourself the goal today to discover at least one new software application that will be important to the programs you supervise. Ask your institution's computer center about new versions of important software programs in your area. Look for important trends in the *Journal of Computer Science and Technology* or the *Journal of Computing in Higher Education*, or a similar publication. Do an Internet search that combines important terms in the disciplines you supervise and phrases such as "computing resources" or "new software packages." Today can be a good time to begin your own education in an application that you've long wanted to know more about, but never found the time for, or to make serious inquiries into applications you've heard about but haven't yet seen in operation. You'll find that many applications can make it easier to accomplish tasks you regard as significant, while others are sure to be valuable for the people who work in the disciplines for which you're responsible.

April 11

❖ *Overplan your day.*

One of the advantages of improving your academic leadership by taking a single small step each day is that it's easy to fit these suggestions into your schedule. You've probably realized by now that even if you added three or four similar tasks to your daily to-do list, you could probably accomplish those without too much difficulty. In fact, unless your schedule is extremely tight, you might be able to squeeze in six or seven such tasks. But what would happen if you gave yourself twenty or twenty-five additional things to do each day? You probably wouldn't get all of them done, but if you made it a special priority and put a lot of energy into the effort, you might accomplish half of them. Even so, ten or twelve completed tasks is a significant achievement, particularly if you thought a moment ago that six or seven extra items a day would require a great deal of work. But sometimes when we overplan a day, we get far more accomplished than we might have done if we'd have settled for merely our ordinary busy pace. So look at your calendar, select a day in the near future that's not already completely filled with meetings and appointments, and then overplan it. Think in terms of small, discrete tasks—or at least small, discrete steps within a larger and more complex task—and schedule yourself to complete twenty or more of those activities in a single day. You won't be able to keep up that pace every day, but as an experiment, it demonstrates just how much you can achieve when you assume you can do more rather than less. By setting your goals high, you'll be able to stretch further than you would otherwise believe.

April 12

❖ *Chart your progress.*

Use today to conduct a quick midcourse check on your progress. Examine your goals and objectives—perhaps focusing on the highest administrative priority that you identified on January 16 or the five short-term goals that you set on January 29—and see how well you're progressing on them. Have you already completed all that you set out to do this year and thus need to set some new goals? Have you at least made a good beginning or developed a practical plan of action? Have you not yet had a chance to start on your goals or perhaps not even given them much thought recently? Candidly assess your progress today and determine whether you're satisfied with the result. If you've met your expectations, congratulate yourself and keep up the good work. If you could've done better, plan how you'll get back on track. Remember that having ambitious goals is a wonderful thing, but they are all but useless if we fail to take the proper steps to achieve them.

April 13

❖ *Check a blind spot.*

We learn things all the time. If you think about it, you'll be able to identify any number of things that you know now but couldn't possibly have known five or ten years ago. Reflect on these learning experiences, and see if you can identify one of them that was particularly important, perhaps even startling. If possible, select something you learned that became so vital to what you do that you can hardly understand how you managed to get by without this knowledge. Next, make a resolution that you'll remember this experience the next time you feel exasperated because someone doesn't know something you think he or she should already have learned. Just like you, your supervisor and the people who work for and with you are in a constant state of discovering new things. Everything we do in our jobs is an opportunity for personal growth and development. Just as we've benefited from our own learning experiences, so do we owe others the right of developing insights at their own pace and in their own ways. Few people are as self-righteous as the person who learned something important five minutes before everyone else. But few sources of pride are as meaningless. By recalling your own blind spots, you'll become a much better example for others since you'll recognize how significant these learning experiences can be.

April 14

❖ *Slow down.*

A great deal of administrative work causes us to hurry. We have deadlines to meet, decisions to make, and crises to resolve. But not everything about our jobs requires that we respond with frantic haste. In fact, there are many things that we would do a whole lot better if we were to slow down, pay attention to all the details, and think matters through. So today, give yourself permission to slow down a bit. Certainly you don't have to proceed through the day as though you were moving in slow motion. But choose one or two projects that you believe could be harmed by excessive rush. Ratchet back your pace a few notches, and take time to explore other possibilities or perspectives. Provide the programs that you supervise with the administrative equivalent of a home-cooked meal as a way of compensating for any "fast food" decisions you may have made in the past.

April 15

❖ *Explore your insecurities.*

Today is the day when people in the United States have to file their federal income tax statements. It's the sort of day that makes a lot of us feel insecure. With this thought in mind, spend some time today considering what you'd regard as your greatest insecurities. What do you fear, or what makes you feel as though you're not in control? Is the first thing that occurs to you the inevitability of death? The possible loss of a loved one? The chance of financial disaster? Public humiliation? Being alone? Something else that's unique to your situation? Being aware of your own insecurities is useful because they can reveal what motivates you, even when you're not always consciously aware of these fears. By reflecting on what makes you uneasy, you may gain insight into why you sometimes react as you do, and even why you make certain professional decisions in a manner that surprises others. As you explore your insecurities, ask yourself, "Why am I concerned about this? Why would that be so bad?" Exploring these issues helps remind us that we all have our insecurities—even the people who report to you and even the people to whom *you* report. Keeping that insight in mind should make you more understanding when others respond in ways that appear inconsistent or irrational.

April 16

❖ *Remember your favorite professor.*

As you recall your own college experience, which professor do you remember most fondly? Nearly all of us have a particularly memorable teacher or mentor who made a lasting difference in our lives. Often this person took an individual interest in us. At other times, our relationship with the professor may have been more distant, but he or she changed the way we looked at ourselves or understood our world. Your favorite professor probably also played at least a small role in guiding you toward your current career. As you reflect on these memories today, enjoy the feelings of nostalgia, but also use today's exercise to recall that everyone has a favorite professor. On your faculty right now, there are people who are changing lives every day and who will long be fondly remembered by the students they serve. In fact, since what people hope to obtain in a professor-student relationship varies so widely, it may well be that every professor who works in your area is somebody's favorite. Keep that possibility in mind today as you interact with your faculty. Remember that you're not just working with people who earn a paycheck; you have the good fortune of working with dedicated professionals who inspire others, improve lives, and build some students' fondest memories.

April 17

❖ *Get excited.*

Some people seem able to be excited about even the most routine events. Others seem incapable of expressing interest in what are truly amazing achievements. Regardless of where you fall on this spectrum, spend some time today identifying at least one thing that excites you in a positive and constructive manner. What do you care about so deeply that when it occurs, it seems as though your whole outlook on life improves? Is there any way that you could bring more of whatever you care about to your life, your job, or your program? Sometimes we get so preoccupied with our efforts to carry out other people's agendas that we forget to include the things that excite us most among our highest priorities. Don't make that mistake today. Get excited about something, and work to incorporate more of it among your daily activities.

April 18

❖ *Identify a significant problem.*

As an academic leader, you play many roles. You represent your programs or possibly even the institution as a whole. You plan for the future. You mentor those who report to you. You evaluate their performance. You work to achieve consensus. And you solve problems. In fact, you probably solve *lots* of problems. Some days it may even feel as though your office serves as the institutional complaint department, with one issue after another dropped in your lap. Of course, many of these problems turn out to be fairly minor. Some of them probably even solve themselves before you get a chance to start looking into them. But other problems are truly severe and require substantial ingenuity to solve. So today, make an effort to identify one of these significant problems. Keep in mind that your goal in this exercise is not to resolve the issue you identify—that's far too ambitious a task for a daily suggestion—but simply to identify it as a major issue to be addressed. With this goal in mind, as you think of the various challenges you face as an academic administrator, which of them seems to be the most serious? That issue can help provide you with a major sense of direction in the days and weeks to come. While you play all the other roles that are included in your administrative profile, you will also be taking steps that move you closer to solving the problem that you identify today.

April 19

❖ *Think like a pilot.*

An old adage of pilots is, "A good flight is any one where you survive the landing." In other words, although there may be many annoyances and petty problems along the way in any journey, the ultimate goal is getting there safely. It's frequently easy to lose perspective in matters of academic administration. Curricular reform often incites rancorous and heated debates. Promotion hearings cause emotions to run high. Almost any significant change can result in passionate arguments. But at the end of the day, the key question for all academic leaders is, "Did we accomplish something important that makes our institution stronger?" If you can honestly answer that question, "Yes. The road may have been difficult, but we achieved something good," then you had a successful flight. In every challenge you face today, don't lose sight of that important insight.

April 20

> ❖ *Jot a note to a member of the staff.*

We saw back on March 4, when you invited a staff member to lunch, just how underpaid and insufficiently appreciated most employees are who work in administrative support areas. Today, continue your efforts to correct this injustice, at least in the case of a single staff member. Identify someone who, in your view, needs encouragement, has done a remarkable job, or made contributions that have long been unrecognized. Send that person a hand-written note of support. Make your comments as personal as possible, reflective of both your values as a supervisor and the employee's contributions as a member of your staff. Don't be surprised if your note is included as part of that person's next annual report or becomes a valued possession. Acknowledgment of a staff member's hard work almost never fails to have a significant and positive impact and is always much appreciated.

April 21

❖ *Chat with a colleague.*

Today, think of someone who holds a position similar to yours at a peer institution. Try to identify someone you know well enough that you will feel comfortable contacting that person just to talk. Call your colleague, and find out what he or she is up to these days. What are the biggest challenges that school is facing? What seems to be his or her most pressing problem? What good news does your friend have to report? Be sure to exchange similar information in kind. Contacts of this sort are valuable because they remind us that we're not as alone as we sometimes believe. There's always someone else who's dealing with issues similar to ours and can provide good advice when we need it. Moreover, if the other person's problems seem worse than your own, you'll have the opportunity to take comfort that your situation doesn't seem quite so bad after all. But if the other person's situation seems far better than yours, then relax and know that your problems are on their way to being solved too; it's all part of the ebb and flow of academic life. Offer your colleague the opportunity to call you anytime to chat, even when no particular reason seems pressing, as a means of staying in touch. You'll find that it's valuable to have frequent access to someone who understands what you're going through.

April 22

❖ *Outline a plan.*

Take a scrap of paper or open a word processing file, and write a single sentence that summarizes your most important goal for the day. If much of the day is still ahead of you, what do you hope to accomplish? What would you be disappointed to leave unfinished if the day ends and this goal is not yet achieved? Then outline a brief but practical plan to accomplish that goal before you leave work. If it's already fairly close to the end of the day when you are reading this entry, how would you summarize what you've achieved since you arrived? Or to put it another way, if someone asked you to articulate what you accomplished, how would you describe it for that person? How did what you do matter to yourself, your discipline, or your institution? If there's something you wanted to accomplish but didn't have time to achieve, outline a short plan to get that task done tomorrow. Many times administrators spend entire days doing a great deal, but take scant time for reflection on how each activity fits into their overall goals. Although that oversight may be unavoidable most days because of the sheer pressure of work, it doesn't have to be true today. By identifying your goal and outlining in a few words your plan to achieve it, you'll find that you stand a much greater chance of accomplishing something substantive and understanding exactly how that task fits into your long-term vision for your institution.

April 23

❖ Walk through your facilities.

You probably spend a lot of time in the building or area where your office is located. Today, make a point of strolling through these facilities with a special purpose: looking for ways in which each area may be unsafe or locations where security could be improved. A few weeks ago, you read over your institution's disaster plan. For today's activity, keep that plan in mind, and imagine it in operation. Are there places where, in the event of a disaster, such items as equipment, doors and windows, or accumulated debris could prove particularly dangerous? Do any exits or passageways have obstructions that should be cleared? Are chemicals and cleaning products stored properly so as not to pose a threat to students and employees? Your institution almost certainly has a designated safety officer or even an entire office charged with protecting environmental health and safety. It's an excellent idea to tour your facilities periodically with someone trained in these matters. That person may be able to point out easy ways in which you can help prevent accidents or avoid citations if your buildings should be inspected by the fire marshal. These periodic walk-throughs are valuable ways to identify and address potential problems and should be one of the regular activities of every academic leader.

April 24

❖ *Live in the moment.*

Many of the suggestions presented in this daily guide prompt you to look toward the past or the future. You're often instructed to reflect on something you already did or to set goals that you'd like to accomplish from this point forward. The reason for this approach is that good academic administration is always highly reflective (the leader seeks to learn something from every experience) and highly intentional (although plans must always remain flexible because of changing circumstances, the leader should always have an idea about what's ahead for the area that he or she supervises). Although these two perspectives are important and necessary, they can cause us to lose sight of the fact that it is always in the present, not the past or the future, that effective administration occurs. In other words, the student to whom we give short shrift because of the meeting that's about to begin didn't receive the full benefit of our academic leadership. The faculty member whose presentation we missed because we were too busy updating the strategic plan was deprived of an opportunity to receive our support. For this reason, a priority today is to be fully engaged in everything you do. Give each meeting, phone call, e-mail, appointment, document, and conversation your complete and undivided attention. You'll have plenty of time to look ahead or to recall the past. (In fact, many of the suggestions you encountered in this book already asked you to do so.) But for today, practice administration by living in each moment as it happens and determining whether that type of approach makes a difference in your overall performance, job satisfaction, or efficiency.

April 25

❖ *Remove your mask.*

Despite our best intentions to the contrary, we frequently wear a mask in our dealings with the world. Perhaps our supervisor insists on moving in a direction about which we have reservations, but we're expected to support that decision anyway. Perhaps we're worried about cuts to our budget and our resulting ability to support recent initiatives, but we still have to demonstrate confidence to our governing board. Or perhaps people ask us every day how we are, and we answer "Fine" almost as a reflex, because we assume people don't really want to know about our frustrations, disappointments, and ailments. While some type of facade is probably inevitable in all interpersonal relationships, we need at least one other person with whom we can be absolutely candid. Today, make it your goal to identify a confidant or trusted mentor with whom you can speak from time to time. When you talk with this person, be frank about your concerns, hopes for the future, doubts, fears, and dreams. Ask for an honest assessment of whether your concerns are justified and if your dreams seem attainable. If your confidant differs substantially from your point of view, don't immediately conclude that you're wrong; simply take some time to reexamine your assumptions. But no matter whether the other person agrees wholeheartedly with you or cautions you away from an idea that you're considering, you'll feel a sense of relief from sharing your candid feelings with someone else.

April 26

❖ *Ask someone about his or her vision.*

As academic administrators, we're always sharing with others our vision for the future of the programs or institution we lead. But today, listen to someone else's vision. Identify a faculty or staff member with whom you haven't had a conversation of this sort, and ask this person, "What would you like to see happen for the future? How would you do things differently? What effects do you think changes could make in our success, and why are these goals important to you?" Your task is not to critique these ideas or even to compare them to your own. Rather, your goal should be simply to listen and try to understand. This conversation could give you a perspective that will help you see your own priorities in a different light. Our individual perspective about a program and its future is frequently dependent on where we stand, and there's a good possibility that you'll have a completely different conversation if you talk to a current student, an alumnus or alumna, a parent, a member of the community nearest your institution, an outstanding teacher, or your most accomplished researcher. None of these outlooks will inherently be right or wrong; they are all simply different. And your own perspective may end up shifting somewhat if you continue to have conversations of this sort.

April 27

❖ *Ask, "What if?"*

Sometimes we get so used to seeing the familiar that we fail to imagine what might be possible. Overcome this limitation by spending a few minutes today visualizing what the future would be like if various things were different. For instance, what would your institution or program be like if:

- Enrollment doubled?
- You had to reduce the size of your faculty by one-third?
- Trends indicated that student credit-hour production in your area was likely to decline steadily over the next decade?
- A natural disaster required you to relocate your entire operation?
- The area you supervise had an opportunity to engage in an exciting but unanticipated area of research?

- A donor's gift paid full tuition, room, and board for all the students in your program or institution?
- Each of the faculty members you supervise had an opportunity to teach or perform research abroad on a Fulbright fellowship?

Develop your own imaginary scenarios as well. This type of thought experiment can alert us to future possibilities by inspiring us to ask, "Well, why not?"

April 28

※ *Indulge your creative side.*

No matter how practical or task oriented an administrator you may be, we all have our creative sides. Not all of us think of ourselves as highly creative, but every time we develop a new idea, solve a problem in an inventive way, or propose a new course, we are engaging in the creative process. Today's task is to indulge your creative side by making a list of the most innovative things you've ever done. When were you able to see a possible solution when others could see only problems? How did you reorganize a curriculum or committee structure in a way that made it more efficient? Did you ever give a presentation that caused others to say afterward, "I never thought of that"? Jot down as many of these experiences as possible, not simply for the pleasure of recalling them but also for reminding yourself of precisely how you've been creative before. Afterward, examine your list to see if you can detect patterns, such as circumstances that tend to feed your creativity. Is there any way that you can recapture or reproduce those conditions? As you encounter the challenges and opportunities that arise in the days to come, remember that you now have evidence of your creative ability to accomplish important goals, and then use that energy to add yet another example of administrative creativity to your list of achievements.

April 29

❖ *Study your students.*

Students come to your program or institution in order to learn what they need in order to achieve their personal goals. So today, spend a few minutes reciprocating the favor: learn more about them. If your office of institutional research can prepare a student profile for you, ask for a copy of this information. Otherwise see what you may be able to gather on your own by calling the admissions office or the director of alumni affairs. Find out what the gender balance is for the students in the area you supervise. What proportion comes from cities or counties located near the school? How many students are from out of state? What percentage of your students are international? Do those who enroll in your program tend to have comparable grade point averages and standardized test scores relative to students in other programs, or is your student population distinctive in some way? What proportion of the student body represents the first generation of their families to attend college? For how many was your school their first choice when they were applying for college? If your program is largely undergraduate in nature, how many of your students expect to attend graduate or professional school? If your administrative assignment involves graduate or professional programs, what percentage of the students in them will pursue a postdoc or secure employment in their chosen career within six months of graduation? The more you know about your current students, the better you'll be able to help recruit others and to assist those who have already enrolled. Knowing the profile of your students will also help you whenever you speak to a potential donor or apply for a grant.

April 30

❖ *Identify your Achilles' heel.*

We all have weaknesses. Sometimes we find it necessary to hide these limitations because we don't want to be taken advantage of or for some other reason. But it's always useful to know all of our weaknesses so that we can compensate for them and, at times, reduce or eliminate them. So, today try to identify your greatest weakness. Perhaps you're not as effective speaking in public as you might like to be. Maybe you don't think quickly on your feet. It could be that you enjoy launching initiatives but lose patience when implementing the details. Possibly you don't share information with others as thoroughly as you could. Whatever the issue may be, be absolutely candid with yourself: find that personal Achilles' heel, and consider what you usually do in order to compensate for your weakness in this area. Then spend some time investigating whether there are more effective ways of dealing with this challenge than the methods you often turn to. Be frank in your assessment as to how your personal limitation puts your institution or program at a disadvantage that it might not have if you didn't possess this weakness.

May

May 1

❖ *Start something.*

May is the month that, at least in the Northern Hemisphere, is commonly associated with the onset of spring. New growth tends to be in evidence all around us. May is also the month when many colleges and universities hold their commencements, a word that (as nearly every graduation speaker relates at some point) refers to the beginning of a new stage in one's life, not the conclusion of an academic program. So today is a fitting time to use this month's emphasis on new growth and fresh starts to initiate a new project of your own. Getting things under way is wonderfully exciting. At the beginning of any process, everything is possible. You haven't yet experienced the frustrations and setbacks that will inevitably occur along the way. Take full advantage of the boundless possibilities that exist, and apply that energy to both your new endeavor and all the other projects that are currently being developed.

May 2

❖ *Evaluate yourself.*

One of the most important responsibilities assigned to academic leaders is evaluating members of the faculty or staff. A well-designed evaluation process can help a poor performer become better and encourage a good performer to become truly excellent. You probably undergo evaluation yourself on a periodic basis, either with your supervisor conducting the process or in a more comprehensive 360-degree manner. But today, take some time to evaluate yourself. Hold yourself to high standards, and don't allow yourself to justify or rationalize the things you haven't done as well as you should. What were your goals for the year, and to what extent have you achieved them? What have been your strengths over the past year? Where did you let yourself or your program down? What advice for improvement would you give if you were a supervisor examining your job performance over the past year? Feel free to take a healthy measure of pride in your achievements, but also acknowledge areas where you should have been more successful. The point of this exercise is not to make yourself feel bad over missed opportunities but to inspire yourself to improve each year in a way that contributes to the strength of your institution and increases your overall job satisfaction.

May 3

❖ *Fill a need.*

All academic administrators exist to fill needs. If a college or university felt that it could operate smoothly without someone performing the tasks you've been assigned, it would be far more efficient to divert your salary to some other area. So even on days when you're feeling that you're not accomplishing much of significance, remember that someone must have felt that your contributions have been useful and that you're probably just being a bit too hard on yourself. Today, invest much of your energy in your role of someone who fills an important need. Identify an unmet priority that you can address either today or at least within a very short time. Then embark on a concentrated effort to fill the need you've identified. The goal of today's activity is not simply to give you a sense of accomplishment for doing something useful, but to help you become more intentional about the way in which you address administrative problems. For instance, how do you go about learning that this particular need exists? Did you rely on your own observation, ask others (if so, whom do you regard as sources of reliable information?), or engage in a more formal and systematic process? Was your first impulse to select a task almost at random from a long list you already have? Were you attracted to a particularly easy task just to get it over with? And how did you go about filling the need itself? Did you break the problem down and consider a variety of solutions? Did you approach it more instinctively or intuitively? Did you rely on the advice of others? Today's activity is an exercise in becoming reflective about the best ways to deal with administrative challenges.

May 4

❖ *Engage in hero worship.*

Who is the person you admire the most? The individual you select could be someone of international prominence whom you've never met or it could be someone local whom you encounter every day. Perhaps you're attracted to another academic leader whose vision or personality seems particularly effective. Perhaps there's a literary character who embodies the values that you hold dear. It doesn't matter where you find your hero, and it's counterproductive to overanalyze your choice. Simply go with your first impression—the first admirable figure who pops into your mind. Then think of a few reasons as to why you admire this person. What qualities does the person have, or what achievements has your hero performed that makes this individual a role model for you? Once you've identified the reasons that you admire the hero you've selected, consider how many of those same qualities you already possess and how many of the hero's achievements you've already had (although perhaps in a different sphere or on a different level). How many of those qualities and achievements would your friends, close colleagues, or members of your family ascribe to you? Most people, when they engage in this thought experiment, discover that they have far more in common with their heroes than they would originally have believed. In other words, we think we have heroes because we want to be like them. In reality, we often choose as our heroes people who are already like us or whom we come to resemble over time. You're already more heroic than you think. So, use this awareness to go out and do something truly heroic today.

May 5

❖ *Spot an elephant.*

We're all familiar with the proverbial elephant in the room. It's the significant issue that everyone knows about, but no one discusses, at least not in public. The elephant in the room is something that's almost taboo for any organization to mention—for example, the possibility that a single-sex institution will go coed, the possibility that the multicampus university will close one of its campuses, the possibility that layoffs and program closures will occur in the face of a budget crisis, and so on—and although it tends to drive a lot of decisions, it rarely appears on the agendas of public meetings. So today, identify the elephant that affects your institution or program and decide that you're not going to ignore it any longer. Resolve that this year will be the time for this issue to be discussed candidly, addressed reasonably, and, if at all possible, resolved completely. Everyone is already aware that this issue is pressing anyway, so why not start dealing with it publicly?

May 6

❧ *Listen actively.*

In everything you address today, make listening your first priority. Don't listen only in the way that you usually do; practice listening with your entire body. When you are engaged in a conversation, lean forward or nod from time to time to indicate that you are following the speaker every step of the way. Use your eyes to suggest that you're open to new ideas. Keep an open posture so that others will realize you're fully engaged. Ask questions—not to challenge other people's ideas or to demonstrate your own command of the issue, but to seek clarification wherever it's needed and to keep the discussion moving forward. Don't agree with anything that you don't honestly support, but don't reject any proposal out of hand. Experiment with how listening can be a matter of not only applying your intellect, but also becoming engaged in a fully visceral and dynamic experience. To be sure, active listening can be exhausting (it is easier sometimes just to tune out a speaker who drones on or repeats information that we already know), but it can also be utterly transforming. Make it an objective today to discover how much more you hear when you decide to listen with more than just your ears.

May 7

❖ *Share a treasure.*

We are who we are because of the values we hold.
Some of our values may be things that motivate us only
tentatively or that we respect only intellectually. But other
principles constitute our core beliefs—the ideals that we
couldn't betray under any circumstances. The very thought
of acting contrary to these values might even make us angry
or disgust us. These values are our treasures, our most cherished beliefs. Today, identify one of these treasures and talk
about it with someone you trust. By articulating the principles that we believe in, we frequently come to understand
them better. Even more important, we come to understand ourselves better, more fully appreciating the reasons
we're so committed to the values we hold dear. By sharing
one of these treasures with someone else today, you'll be
illustrating your strong commitment to this principle, and
you'll find that you come to embody it more and more in
your life. Why? Well, once you've revealed that this particular value is truly significant for you, others will begin
to expect it to be demonstrated through your actions, and
you'll come to expect it of yourself as well. After all, you
wouldn't want to be hypocritical by giving a core belief lip-
service but then violating it in how you behave. So, select
your treasure carefully, but then share it confidently.

May 8

❖ *Reward others.*

Even if you work at the most dysfunctional institution imaginable, there must be at least one of your employees whose success continues to impress you and others in your program. The person you identify today should be someone who consistently goes above and beyond the demands of the job to provide truly excellent service. Think about the rewards you have available, and find some way of acknowledging this person's contributions. The reward need not be monetary—you may even work in an environment where bonuses or salary differentials are not available—as long as it is significant for the person involved. Public recognition, a title change, a better office, an improvement in responsibilities, or an extra day off can all serve as effective rewards. Consider the incentives you can offer people, and select something that is appropriate for both the type of contribution the person has made and his or her own needs, interests, and desires.

May 9

❖ *Reorganize a drawer.*

The longer we hold our administrative positions, the more disorganized our desk usually becomes. Our desk drawers become receptacles for items we won't ever need again, and their initial state of order soon degenerates into a cluttered mess where even useful items are all but impossible to find. Improve this situation today by choosing one drawer to reorganize. If your desk has remained relatively neat, then select a drawer in a file cabinet, credenza, or cupboard in your office area. Keeping in mind all institutional policies about how long important records need to be retained, try to identify documents that are no longer necessary and can safely be discarded or shredded. Be careful to dispose properly of papers that include confidential information, such as Social Security numbers or student grades. For items that are worth retaining, consider whether your desk drawer is their proper place. How can the papers you need be reorganized so as to make them more useful and accessible to you? Taking one small step toward reorganizing your workspace will help apply greater focus to the entire day. Although some administrators scoff at the idea, most people work more effectively in a neat and attractive environment. Regard today's exercise in reorganization as but a single step along a path that leads toward making your whole job more systematic, efficient, and productive.

May 10

❖ *Reflect on the law of reciprocity.*

Have you ever noticed that the people who treat others angrily or dismissively frequently find their world to be an angry and dismissive place? People who expect confrontation generally find it, while those who act calmly, openly, and reasonably usually discover that other people are calm, open, and reasonable. The law of reciprocity says that the way in which we engage others tends to be the way in which they treat us in return. We don't need to believe in karma or to elevate this law into a cosmic principle to understand why we tend to reap what we sow. We are constantly modeling for other people how we expect them to treat us. We change situations by making them more negative through anger and hostility or calmer and more productive through rationality and understanding. If you often find that the people around you are treating you in ways that you don't find constructive, reflect on the way in which you're interacting with them in order to determine whether, on even the slightest level, you've introduced a type of negative energy that's now being returned to you because of the law of reciprocity.

May 11

❖ *Use your resources.*

Whenever you start a new project, it's very easy to think that you will need to begin at the very beginning. For example, if you have to develop a new policy, your initial impulse may be to believe that you need to start with an in-depth study of the problem that must be solved, consult with all the stakeholders who are affected by the issue, propose several possible solutions, collate responses to the various possibilities that have been suggested, and then discuss them until consensus is achieved or a vote can be held to decide the matter. Certainly we all have problems that need to be addressed in precisely that way. But for an amazing number of issues in higher education, effective models and best practices already exist and can be adapted to your specific situation. Among the many resources that you have available to you are the lessons you can learn from your peers at other institutions. For this reason, today's task is to select an issue with which you're currently dealing. Identify a few appropriate keywords, and do an Internet search to discover how other colleges and universities approach this matter. Call one or two colleagues at other schools, and ask how they deal with this problem in their programs. For particularly complex issues, go through the programs of administrative conferences related to your level of responsibility and see whether there are presentations or panels on this issue. Search the Web sites of publishers that specialize in college administration. You will use your time much more efficiently by borrowing and adapting from others than if you try to reinvent the wheel for every challenge that comes your way.

May 12

❖ *Describe your coworkers.*

Take a sheet of scratch paper or open a computer file and jot down every descriptive phrase that comes to your mind when you think of the people who report to you.

Don't stop this exercise until you're completely out of ideas. Next, draw a line on the paper or insert a page break into your electronic document and do the same thing for your peers—the people who hold positions similar to yours. Finally, use a third section to describe how you feel about your own supervisor or the governing board of your institution. When your lists are complete, go through them, placing a plus sign before any phrase that seems positive or complimentary, a minus sign before any phrase that seems negative, and a zero before any phrase that's merely descriptive without being particularly positive or negative. Then reflect on whether your descriptions are mostly positive, mostly negative, mostly neutral, or evenly balanced for each group. No matter the outcome of this exercise, it should give you some indication of your true feelings about your coworkers. Even if you're excellent at concealing your emotions, those reactions are probably already known to the people you've just described. People pick up on subtle visual and verbal cues about our reactions to them. The result can be a vicious cycle. In other words, when a colleague does something that you regard as foolish, you may begin treating that person like a fool and, as a result, he or she will probably live up (or down) to your expectations. If you reframe your thoughts and raise your expectations, you may end up surrounded by people who begin appearing far wiser, more competent, and less problematic.

May 13

✢ *Become disillusioned.*

When most people speak about being disillusioned, they regard this state as wholly negative. They use the word *disillusioned* as a synonym for *cynical* or *disheartened*, and feel that the world has let them down somehow. In fact, the literal meaning of *disillusioned* is being freed from your illusions—those false beliefs and erroneous assumptions that can cause you to live in a fantasy world rather than reality. Even if our fantasies are charming, aren't we better off dealing with the world as it is rather than remaining in a fool's paradise? Today's exercise is thus to consider several of the premises and assumptions that guide your behavior and then to identify whether any of them may be an illusion. Your personal illusion may be your repeated hope that a situation's going to change despite all the evidence to the contrary. Or it could be a career goal that, if you were honest with yourself, you'd admit you are likely never to attain and that's diverting far too much energy and attention from your current responsibilities. Your illusion could be a realization that someone who appears to be supporting you actually does not have your best interests at heart. The point is that we all have illusions, but we will make genuine progress as academic leaders only when we set these phantoms aside and begin to deal with the reality of our situations.

May 14

❖ *Learn something new about budgeting.*

Even small schools have surprisingly complex budgets. In part, this situation occurs because colleges and universities are so wonderfully multifaceted. They include many different types of employees, from faculty members and researchers to clerical workers and administrators to librarians and business managers to maintenance personnel and groundskeepers. Then there's also the complexity of the physical plant: residence halls, classrooms, laboratories, art studios and galleries, performance spaces, practice rooms, meeting rooms, and offices. Depending on whether the school is public or private, a different set of budgetary policies will be in effect, and these policies are likely not to be the same as those you're familiar with if you ever worked in a different state. Rules for purchasing, leasing, implementing grants, conducting sponsored research, and borrowing equipment are often quite complicated, as can be the restrictions on how funds must be donated and their expenditures monitored. Like assessment and strategic planning, budgets are one of the areas about which administrators simply can't know too much. So, make it your goal today to gain at least one new major insight into how budgets are prepared, structured, or implemented at your college or university. If what you learn applies to your own area, this knowledge will help you almost immediately make better budgetary decisions. If what you learn applies more globally to the institution or to higher education as a whole, then you'll at least gain a better understanding of the overall budget-building process and possibly lay important groundwork for your next administrative position.

May 15

⋙ *Make up for lost time.*

Your academic year is either over or soon will be. There are probably many things you intended to do this year but never quite got around to. (Think, for instance, of New Year's resolutions.) Even if you began working with this guide on September 1 with the intention of following every single suggestion on the very day it was proposed, you are likely to have overlooked several of them. One date may have fallen on a weekend or some other time when your institution was not in session. Another suggestion may have fallen on a date when you were out of town or too busy to take on one more task—even a small one. Life gets busy, especially for academic leaders. So today's the day to make up for lost time. Go through the first part of this book, select one of the suggestions that you haven't yet followed, and do it today. The idea isn't simply to have a makeup day but also to illustrate an important principle: you can take this same approach toward many other missed opportunities in either your current job or your overall career. We sometimes believe that once we make a decision to proceed in a certain direction, all other directions are closed to us. But that's rarely true. Today's opportunity to make up for lost time serves as a good reminder of other ways in which you can now do something you should have done earlier. The simple fact is that sometimes all it takes to recover a lost possibility is to decide that you've already spent far too much time and are now finally prepared to take the action you've long believed was right.

May 16

❖ *Audit your organizational structure.*

An old joke about academic administration goes, "How many assistant deans does it take to screw in a light bulb?" The answer to this riddle is, "One more than last year," and you could easily revise the joke to relate to staff members at any level of the institution. Many faculty members remain skeptical of the need for ever larger organizational structures when, in their view, they are constantly being asked to take on more responsibilities with fewer and fewer rewards. In light of this common sentiment, it's a good practice to audit your organizational structure from time to time, asking whether duties that exist in your area justify the number of staff positions you have and whether the right people are being assigned to the right tasks. At times, administrative staffs are expanded because the individuals who hold those positions have certain limitations, abilities, or temperaments. As those individuals move on to other jobs, an organizational structure that made sense once no longer seems logical or appropriate. So every year, academic leaders should audit their administrative staffs to make sure that tasks are being done correctly and in a timely manner, existing full-time positions truly warrant full-time staffing, and levels of assignment are equitable in terms of the compensation the employees receive. Changes as the result of an organizational audit can be extremely difficult to make, but they can also have a profoundly positive effect on both morale and efficiency if they are made properly.

May 17

❖ *Practice concision.*

Academic leaders communicate in many different ways. They write letters and e-mails, make speeches, welcome guests, mingle with participants at various events, interact one-on-one with faculty members and students in appointments, and create many other kinds of documents and public presentations. But effective administrative communication is almost always concise. Please note, however, that the word *concise* here should not be taken to mean "abrupt" or "terse." There's a broad spectrum of possibilities between answering an e-mail with a single word (or even not answering it at all) and crafting a reply that goes on for several thousand words. Concise communication provides the efficiency we all need in order to handle the workload that is involved in academic leadership. As a result, in speeches and formal presentations, the old adage, "Always leave them wanting more," remains excellent advice. Remember that no one ever left an auditorium wishing that the speech of a dean or provost had been longer. In e-mails and letters too, it is possible to be warm and personable in only a sentence or two. Today, try to attain this type of concision in all of your communications. Whenever you're writing someone or engaged in a conversation, get directly to the point, and by the end of the day, you'll see how many issues you were able to deal with effectively, quickly, and well.

May 18

❖ *Brag about someone.*

Make it a point today to speak in glowing terms about a member of your faculty or staff. In fact, spread your attention around a little bit. Select a different person from the person you thanked on January 3, whose good news you celebrated on February 10, or whom you took to lunch on March 4. In the best of all circumstances, the person you talk about today should not even be in earshot when you make your remarks. Sometimes the comments that make us feel worst are those that someone says behind our backs, and the remarks that give us the greatest pleasure are the compliments bestowed on us when we're not around. We know then that the praise wasn't given simply because we happened to be there, and yet the remarks that others make always seem to find their way back to us. In performing today's suggestion, you can be sure that your good words will get back to the person you're complimenting. You probably have many deserving employees to choose from: the member of the staff who puts in many hours of work off the clock, the faculty member who goes out of his or her way to help a student, the researcher who is motivated solely by the hope of helping others. In fact, when you think of all the good work these people have done, having only one day to brag about them hardly seems enough.

May 19

❖ *Read about academic leadership.*

The more we learn about effective and creative ways of doing our jobs, the better administrators we become. For this reason, try to find a book about some aspect of college administration that interests you. Look for a resource that deals with a topic you don't know as much about as you probably should—perhaps an issue like assessment, curricular development, faculty and staff evaluation, diversity and multiculturalism, faculty roles and rewards, instructional technology, cooperative agreements with local industry, mentoring, or service-learning. You might even consider selecting a book on the theory and practice of academic leadership itself. Your experience will probably be best if you select a very recent book, since new research is being done all the time, and ideas develop rapidly in higher education. See if the ideas contained in the book can help you achieve some of your goals or solve some of your problems. We never finish learning everything we need to know as academic administrators, and discovering new books on topics that we haven't yet mastered helps keep our approaches fresh as we face the many responsibilities of our positions.

May 20

❖ *Resist the temptation to be cynical.*

Good administrators are always skeptical but never cynical. Being skeptical means that you rely on evidence, rather than guesswork or blind conviction, when you decide what's right and wrong. Being cynical means that you automatically assume the worst, frequently believing that others are motivated only by what they stand to gain themselves. Cynical administrators are suspicious, pessimistic, distrustful, and frequently contemptuous of others. One repeated theme that we saw back on October 15 and May 12 was that people often live up or down to our expectations of them.

If you assume that most people are out to cheat you, you'll create an environment in which that type of dishonesty regularly occurs. But if you assume that most people are trying to do what they believe is right, not only for themselves but also for those whom they serve, you'll create a positive and collegial academic environment. You probably play a much larger role in setting the tone of your unit or institution than you even imagine. As an academic leader, you have the responsibility to resist the urge to be cynical and, in so doing, to improve that tone immensely.

May 21

❖ *Be a good public citizen.*

One important responsibility of every academic leader is serving as an advocate for the people who report to you. If you're a chair, you must be the voice of your department. If you're a dean, you're expected to defend the interests of your college. If you're a president, you must do everything you can to promote the institution that you lead, and so on. But counterbalancing your role as an advocate is the expectation that you must also be a good public citizen in the broadest possible sense. You have to be able to see the larger picture to understand how your unit fits into the overall scheme of the institution or how your institution fits into the broader realm of higher education in general. Today's task therefore is to devote some time to meeting your obligations as a good public citizen. Look after the needs of those who depend on you, of course, but also ask yourself how your program's priorities relate to goals, needs, and aspirations of an enterprise that's larger than your unit alone. Keep in mind that sometimes the best way to serve your own self-interest is to serve the interests of others first.

May 22

❖ *Define who you are.*

If you were to complete the sentence, "I'm a ...," what are the first words that would come to mind? Do you define yourself primarily in terms of your job, your accomplishments, your family, your gender or ethnicity, your place of origin, your appearance, or some other factor? What does it reveal about you that one particular description popped into your head as soon as you began to think about who you are? How might you be conveying that self-image to others in the way that you act or speak? Understanding who you are is an important prerequisite to making any sort of improvement or development in leadership. Just as it's extremely difficult to arrive anywhere if you're not even sure where you started from, so you increase the difficulty of making progress as an academic leader if you don't begin with a certain degree of self-awareness. As you conduct today's thought experiment, don't judge yourself too harshly, condemning flaws or wallowing in regrets. At the same time, don't waste time congratulating yourself for your successes. Rather, merely assess who you are critically and objectively. Then decide which of these factors in your identity helps you succeed as an academic leader and which makes your job more challenging. In the weeks ahead, set the goal of expanding the former, while working to compensate for or (where possible) eliminate the latter.

May 23

❖ *Pay it forward.*

When someone we know does us a favor, we often pay it back at some point in the future. For instance, suppose that your car's in the shop and a colleague gives you a ride home; later, when that colleague is similarly in need of a ride, you're probably going to provide one in turn. But some favors are impossible to pay back: the mentor who once secured an interview for us with a phone call, the boss who demonstrated restraint and understanding when we made a serious mistake, the professor who allowed us to complete a course when we couldn't attend class due to a prolonged illness. We'll probably never be in a position to pay those people back in the same way that they helped us. At least, we're unlikely to be able to pay them back in any meaningful way. Our best approach in such a case is to pay the favor forward. In other words, we can decide to help someone who has a need similar to the one we once had. Paying it forward helps administrators maintain a humane and charitable approach to academic leadership even on those days when the problems seem numerous, everyone appears to be upset about something, and it seems all but impossible that we will ever make a lasting difference.

May 24

❖ *Take a calculated risk.*

Some of the most important improvements that administrators in higher education can effect pose some element of risk. Academic leaders can't make every decision only after they conduct a thorough cost-benefit analysis, review the proposal with focus groups, and consult every possible stakeholder. Sometimes being entrepreneurial means trusting your instincts and taking a chance. No capable administrator would willingly accept the type of risk that could put his or her entire program or institution at stake. But smaller gambles can often lead to impressive results. With these thoughts in mind, make it your goal today to identify a calculated risk that you would be willing to take. Try to choose an endeavor that would be highly beneficial if it works out but would produce consequences you can live with if it doesn't. You don't have to implement the entire idea today; merely identify it, start planning for it, and commit to taking the risk. Significant advances in academic programs often do not come about because of small, incremental changes but because of the very type of bold resolution that you'll be making today.

May 25

❖ *Assess your network.*

We all have a network of people on whom we rely for support and guidance. Your own network might include members of your family, coworkers, colleagues at other institutions, friends, mentors, acquaintances, and even a few friendly competitors. Today's activity is to assess this network and consider whether it is as effective as it might be. Do you tend to expect more from others than you usually give in return? Do you make a concerted effort to expand your system of contacts whenever you attend conferences and meet other people? Do you view your network from a very calculating perspective, seeing the value of the people you know only in terms of what they can do for you? Or do you find, to the contrary, that you often feel used by the relationships that others have tried to develop with you? Evaluate both your network itself and your skills in developing this network of contacts from the perspective of how your personal support group helps you to advance professionally, encourages you to grow personally, and provides you with opportunities to be of service to those who can benefit from your unique skills.

May 26

❖ *Set a clear development goal.*

Fundraising and the cultivation of people who support your program or institution can provide inconsistent results. One year you might secure an extremely large gift and attract numerous new members of the community to your events. The very next year could be a complete disaster in terms of raising new funds, and people may seem to be interested in everything else but the programs and events your area is able to offer. Despite this unpredictability—or perhaps because of it—it's important for every academic leader to set clear development goals. Today's activity is to set one of these goals, perhaps related to the amount of external funding you still hope to receive by the end of the fiscal year or perhaps concerning your ambitious plans for the next fiscal or academic year. Whichever you choose, set the bar high enough that you'll be challenged and compelled to be innovative in order to reach your goal. But don't be so idealistic or impractical that you have no chance whatsoever to accomplish what you propose. For instance, if you've never been involved in advancement activities before, setting a multimillion-dollar fundraising goal and the objective of identifying several thousand new community supporters is almost certainly unrealistic. After all, you want to stretch, not break, as you strive to meet this challenge. But without being highly motivated, it will be difficult to sustain the commitment you'll need to attain great things on days when the pressure of immediate deadlines seems far more urgent. Clear, impressive, and publicly announced goals can be highly motivating since you won't want to fail at a task that you described as very important to you.

May 27

❖ *Change your inner voice.*

Having an inner voice is quite a different thing from hearing voices in your head. Your inner voice is what either cheers you on or tells you, "You'll never make it," when you're trying something difficult. It's not a hallucination— something that urges you to do something dangerous or contrary to your values; it's the way in which you give yourself advice, define your relationship with the world, and attempt to view yourself as you imagine others see you. Today's suggestion is to make a conscious effort to change some aspect of your inner voice so that it'll be more helpful to you. Reprogram the negative advice you give yourself into more encouraging or positive statements. For example, if you find yourself saying things like, "You're no good at this" (whatever "this" is), always be sure to add, "but I'm getting better at it all the time." If you find yourself thinking negatively of others or distrusting their motives, alter your inner voice to say, "Still, I know we're all doing the best we can in an imperfect situation, with limited resources, and filled with anxieties about our own futures." You can start this exercise by thinking of at least five positive things to say about anyone toward whom you usually feel contempt or antipathy—even if that person happens to be yourself. An old customer service technique says that if you smile whenever you answer the phone, the other person will "hear" that smile in your voice. For today, therefore, see if you can count all the ways in which, when your inner voice is "smiling" kindly as it speaks to you, you will become a better and more effective academic leader.

May 28

❖ *Learn from the fragments of broken promises.*

Try as we might, there are times when we're unable to keep our word. Situations change. Unexpected problems arise. Human frailty intervenes. Or we simply forget about a promise that seemed insignificant to us but turned out to matter a great deal to someone else. For good administrators, these occurrences are relatively rare. Effective academic leaders take their commitments seriously and want their promises to be something that everyone can count on. But today, reflect on a situation when you were unable to keep your word or, worse, simply neglected to do so. What were the implications? What lessons did you learn from what occurred? If there are still problems lingering from this incident, are there steps you can take now to remedy them? Even if the incident occurred so long in the past that no further reparation is possible or necessary, examining the fragments of a broken promise has tremendous value. It reminds us that these unfortunate circumstances occur and that sometimes *we are the ones responsible*. That insight helps us to be more understanding and to respond more constructively the next time we are the person to whom a broken promise has been made.

May 29

❖ *Build outward from individual successes.*

A benefit of working through a year-long guide like this one is that it causes you to try many different things, some of which you may not have attempted without the encouragement of each day's suggestion. Inevitably, however, some of the ideas in this book will have appealed to you more than others, and the specific activities that you find most helpful may well be different from those another administrator regards as valuable. So as the academic year comes to a close, it's time to reflect on the suggestions you've encountered in this book and decide which of them you'd like to make a regular part of your administrative routine. Which suggestions do you want to return to in the coming year, building on the individual successes of a single day so that they'll become an ongoing part of your administrative approach? Identify a small and manageable number of the activities and suggestions you encountered here—perhaps no more than ten or twelve—and resolve to make them part of your daily routine. If it's helpful to do so, place these tasks periodically on your calendar in order to provide you with an ongoing reminder until they become second nature. Remember that an activity tried only once remains merely an experiment, but an activity you do continually becomes part of who you are.

May 30

❖ *Reinvent the wheel.*

Earlier this month, we saw the importance of using your resources since effective models and best practices already exist and can be easily adapted to your specific situation. While that is certainly practical advice in most situations, there are also times when administrators are better off planning from scratch and not being unduly influenced by the example of others. That is, if every college or university simply followed a procedure developed elsewhere, no new best practices would ever emerge. We'd still be using the same models of curricular development, administrative structure, and research support that institutions had in place many decades ago. For this reason, select today some aspect of your administrative planning where you believe that it's absolutely impossible to do things in the same way as others or to approach a problem in the manner that most other schools do. Where, in other words, is it beneficial for your program or institution to cease following the examples that are in place elsewhere and begin thinking in a new way that's right for your unique situation? You may well discover that it's only by ceasing to follow certain trends that we have any hope of becoming trendsetters ourselves.

May 31

⟡ *Start your own daily guide.*

As you've read each daily entry throughout this year, you've undoubtedly developed your own ideas of thought experiments, activities, or advice that could help other academic leaders. (And admit it: you probably thought, "Oh, I could've come up with a better suggestion than *that*!" on at least a few days.) Well, today's the day to put your money where your mouth is. Set yourself the goal of writing your own daily guide to academic leadership over the coming year. At the start of each day, write down a thought or idea that you believe would be of interest to other administrators. When the year is over and your guide is complete, share it with others. Publish it through an established press or use one of the many excellent self-publishing firms. Distribute your thoughts online as a Web site. In fact, if you start recording your suggestions in a blog, you won't have to wait a full year to distribute it: post the first entry tomorrow, and then add a new idea each day throughout the coming months. By setting yourself this task and sticking to it, you'll become even more intentional about your work as an academic leader, and your program and stakeholders will benefit in the process. All of us who are committed to the notion that small steps can lead to great success need to stick together. Feel free to share your own suggestions and advice with me at jeffbuller@me.com and let me know the secrets of academic administration you've discovered along the way. Have a fantastic summer!

The Author

Jeffrey L. Buller is dean of the Harriet L. Wilkes Honors College of Florida Atlantic University. He began his administrative career as honors director and chair of the Department of Classical Studies at Loras College in Dubuque, Iowa, before going on to assume a number of administrative appointments at Georgia Southern University and Mary Baldwin College. Buller is the author of *The Essential College Professor: A Practical Guide to an Academic Career* (2010), *The Essential Academic Dean: A Practical Guide to College Leadership* (2007), *The Essential Department Chair: A Practical Guide to College Administration* (2006), *and Classically Romantic: Classical Form and Meaning in Wagner's Ring* (2001). He has written numerous articles on Greek and Latin literature, nineteenth- and twentieth-century opera, and college administration. From 2003 to 2005, Buller served as the principal English-language lecturer at the International Wagner Festival in Bayreuth, Germany. An active consultant to the Sistema Universitario Ana G. Méndez in Puerto Rico and the Ministry of Higher Education in Saudi Arabia, where he holds the position of adjunct professor of academic development at King Fahd University of Petroleum & Minerals, Buller is widely known as an entertaining and popular speaker on such topics as international culture, music, literature, and higher education.

Index

R

S

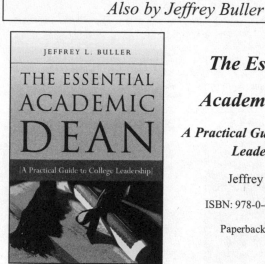

The Essential

Academic Dean

A Practical Guide to College Leadership

Jeffrey Buller

ISBN: 978-0-470-18086-0

Paperback | 448 pp.

The role of an academic dean is extremely complex, involving budgeting, community relations, personnel decisions, managing a large enterprise, mastering numerous details, fundraising, and guiding a school or college toward a compelling vision for the future. But no academic dean can quickly master all of the intricacies involved in this challenging position. For instance, how do you build support for a shared vision of your unit's future? How do you interact effectively with all of the different internal and external constituencies that a dean must serve? How do you set, supervise, and implement a budget? How do you handle the volume of documents that cross your desk? How do you fire someone, ask a chair to step down, respond to a reporter on the telephone, and settle disputes about intellectual property rights? How do you know when it's time to consider leaving your current position for another opportunity?

The Essential Academic Dean is about the "how" of academic leadership. Based on a series of workshops given by the author on college administration and management, each topic deals concisely with the most important information deans need at their fingertips when faced with a particular challenge or opportunity. Written both as a comprehensive guide to the academic deanship and as a ready reference to be consulted when needed, this book emphasizes proven solutions over untested theories and stresses what deans need to know now in order to be most successful as academic leaders.

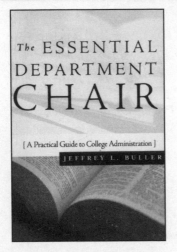

The Essential Department Chair

A Practical Guide to College Administration

Jeffrey Buller

ISBN: 978-1-882982-99-8

Paperback | 312 pp.

There are many guides for academic administrators that explore differing philosophies of administration, theoretical approaches to management and leadership, and new trends in higher education administration. Books such as these can inspire department chairs to develop a major new vision for their discipline or even their entire institution. But in order to make that vision a reality, chairs must know how to excel at the many administrative tasks assigned to them. For instance, how do you cultivate a potential donor for much-needed departmental resources? How do you interview someone when your dean assigns you to a committee searching for an administrator in a different academic area? How do you fire someone? How do you get your department members to work together more harmoniously? How do you keep the people who report to you motivated and capable of seeing the big picture?

The Essential Department Chair is about the "how" of academic administration. Based on a series of workshops given by the author in the area of faculty and administrative development, each topic deals concisely with the most important information chairs will want to have at their fingertips when faced with a particular challenge or opportunity. Intended to be a ready reference that chairs turn to as needed, this book emphasizes proven solutions over untested theories and stresses what chairs need to know now in order to be most successful in their administrative positions.

The Essential College Professor

A Practical Guide to an Academic Career

Jeffrey Buller

ISBN: 978-0-470-37373-6

Paperback | 432 pp.

College professors are expected to perform a large number of tasks for which they receive little or no training. For instance, where in graduate school do you learn how to teach most effectively in a large auditorium, and what do you do differently in those classes from when you are teaching in a more intimate setting, with a few upper-level students around a seminar table or in a tutorial? How do you go about applying for external funding to support your research? How do you write a particularly effective syllabus or exam? How do you create the sort of curriculum vitae that is most likely to earn you tenure, promotion, another position, or an administrative appointment? How do you chair a committee? How do you deal with a student who is disrupting one of your classes? Why should you engage in fundraising, recruiting new students, or maintaining close ties with alumni? Why should you develop a "strategic plan" for your career, improving your teaching and enhancing your research?

The Essential College Professor is about the "how" and "why" of being a faculty member in higher education today. Based on the author's series of highly successful faculty development workshops, each chapter deals concisely with the most important information college professors need at their fingertips when confronted by a particular challenge or faced with an exciting opportunity. Written both as a comprehensive guide to an academic career and as a ready reference to be consulted when needed, *The Essential College Professor* emphasizes proven solutions over untested theories and stresses what faculty members need to know now in order to be successful in their careers.